Test Color

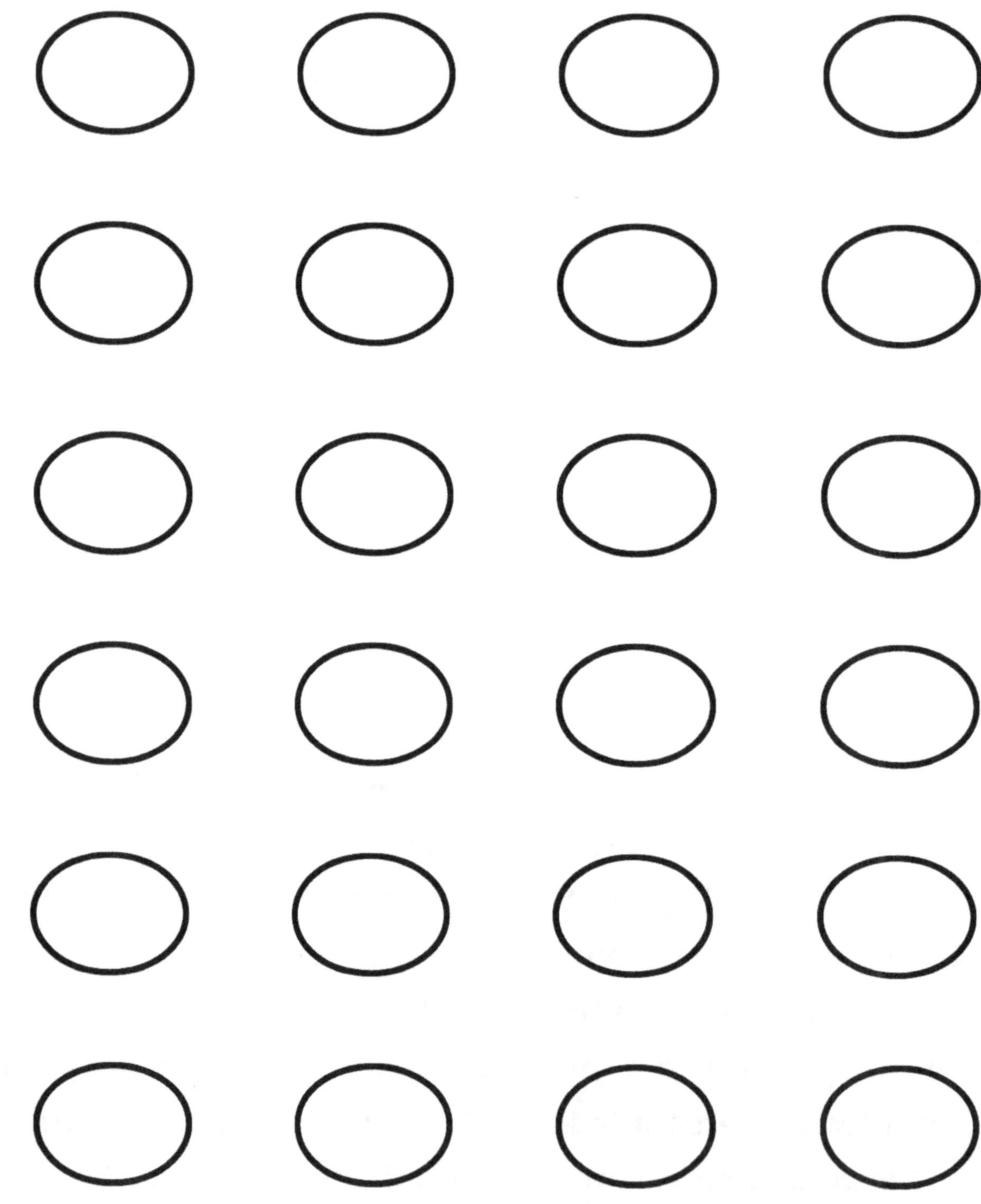

Test Color

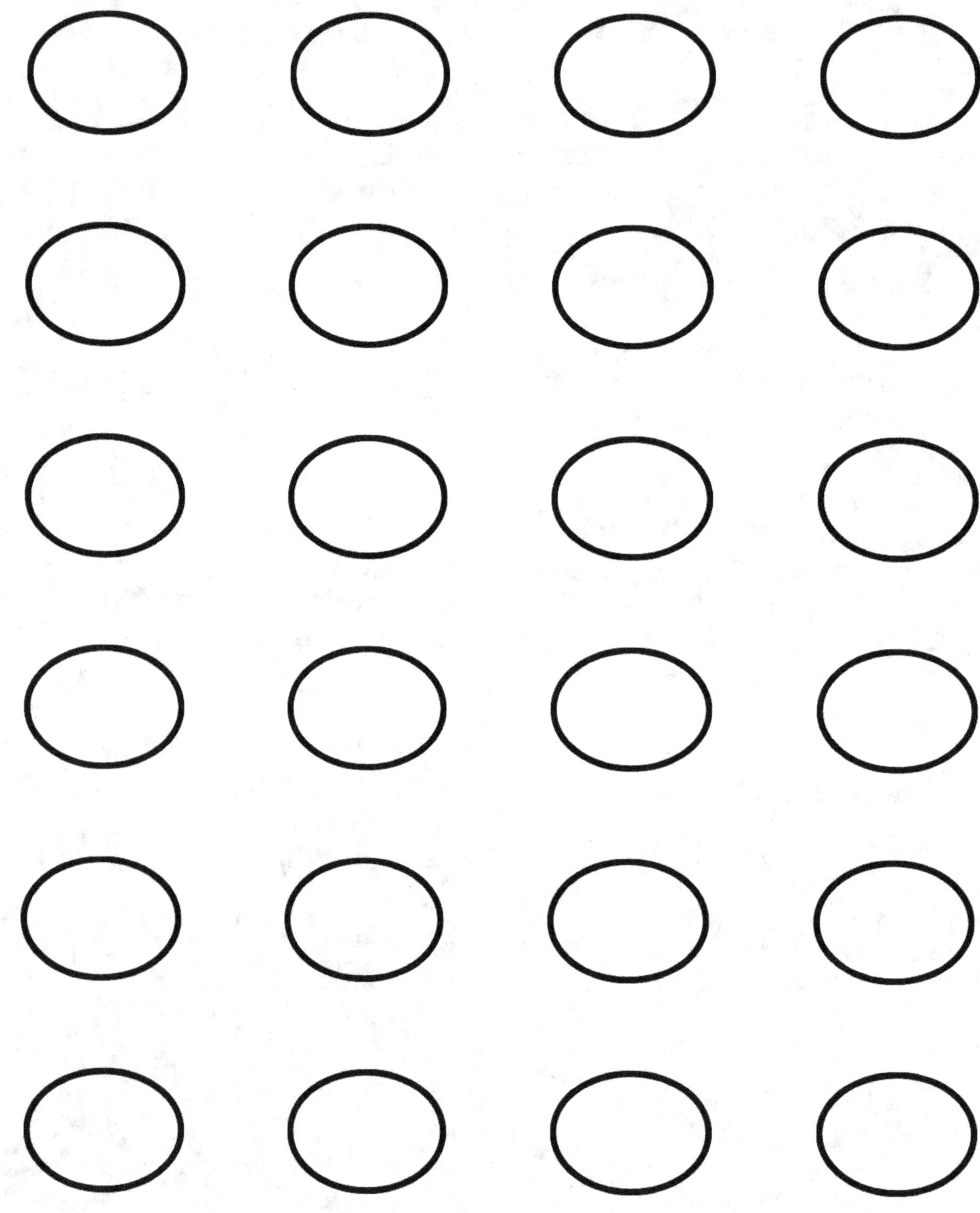

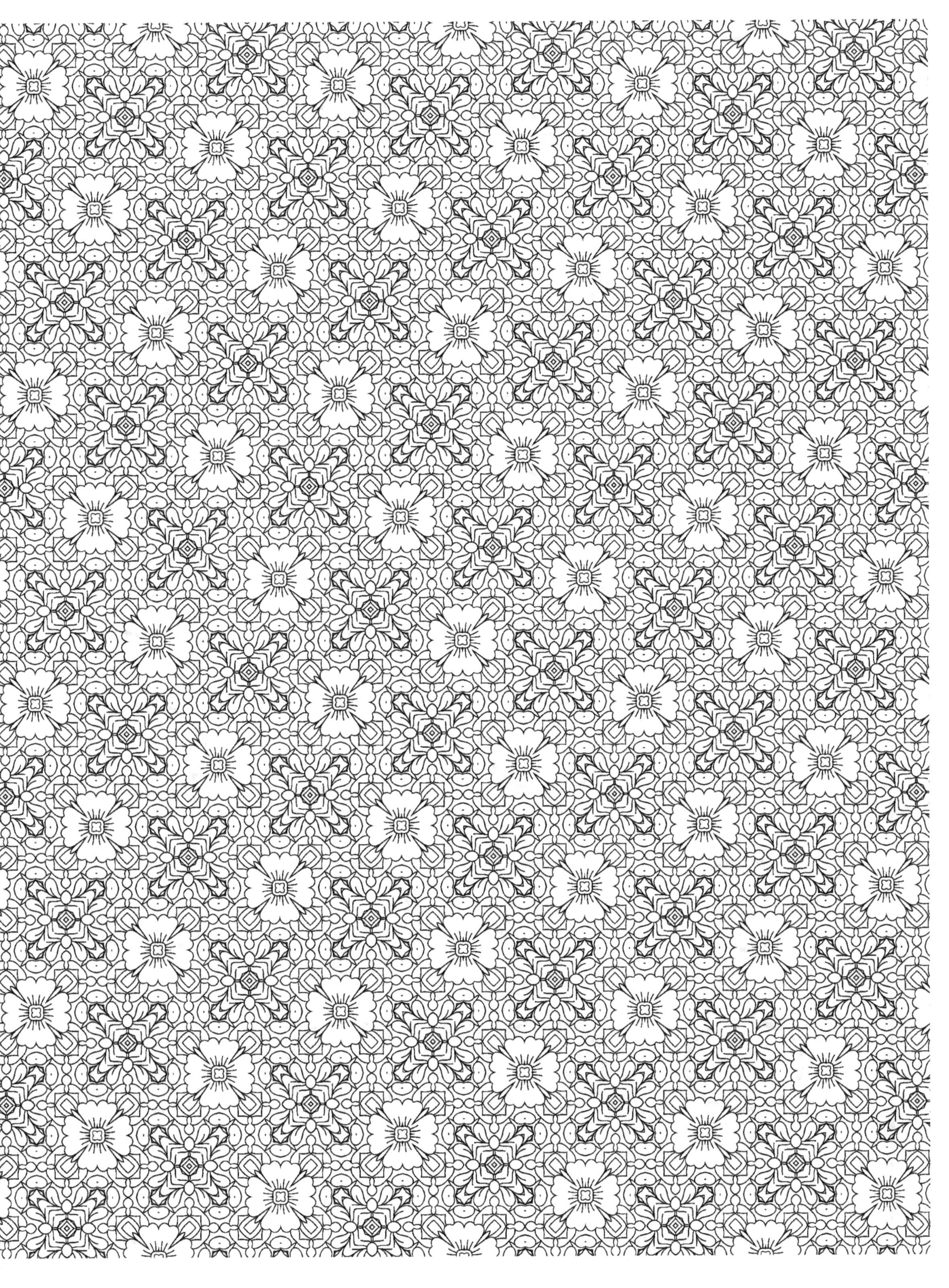

Test Color

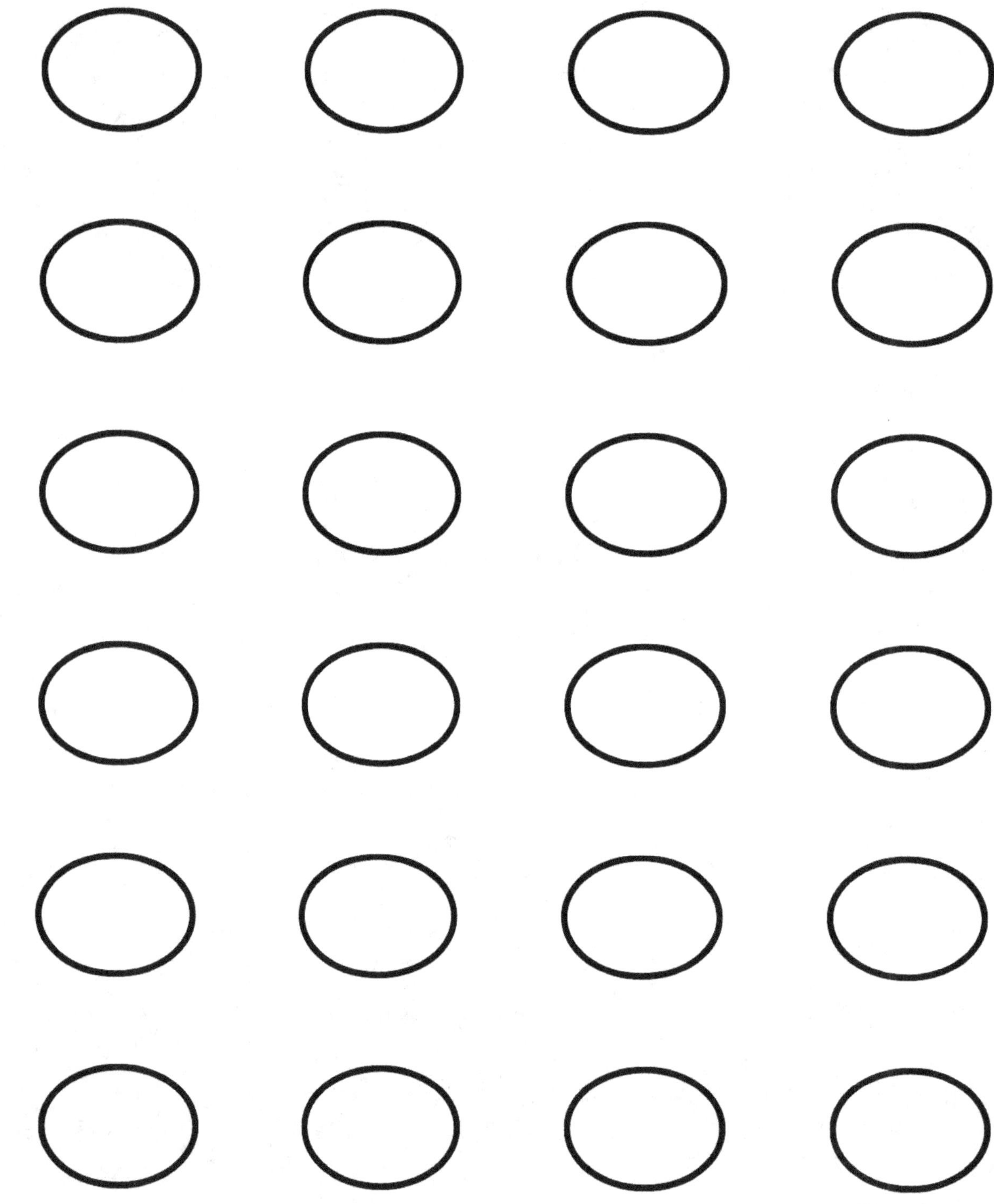

Test Color

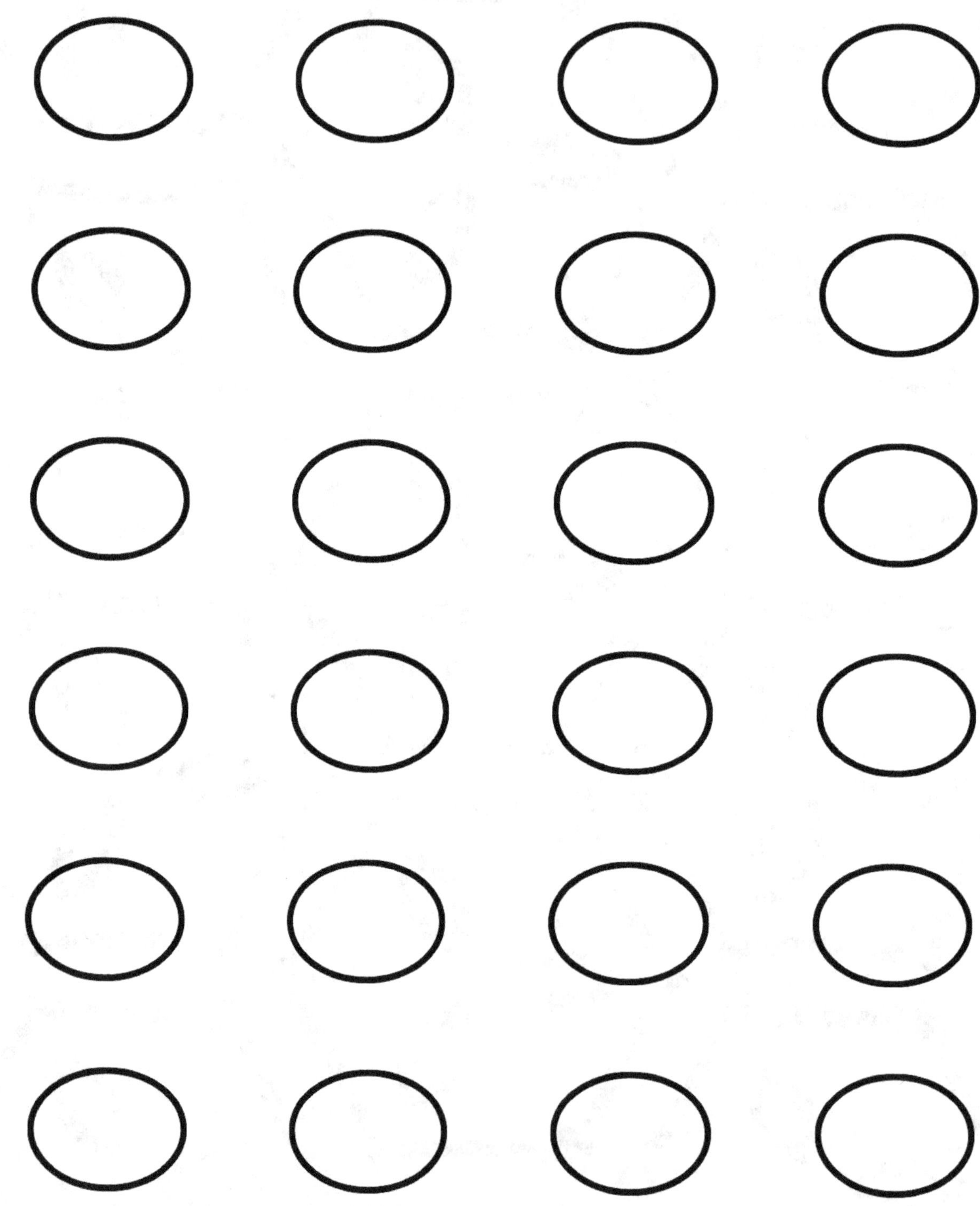

Test Color

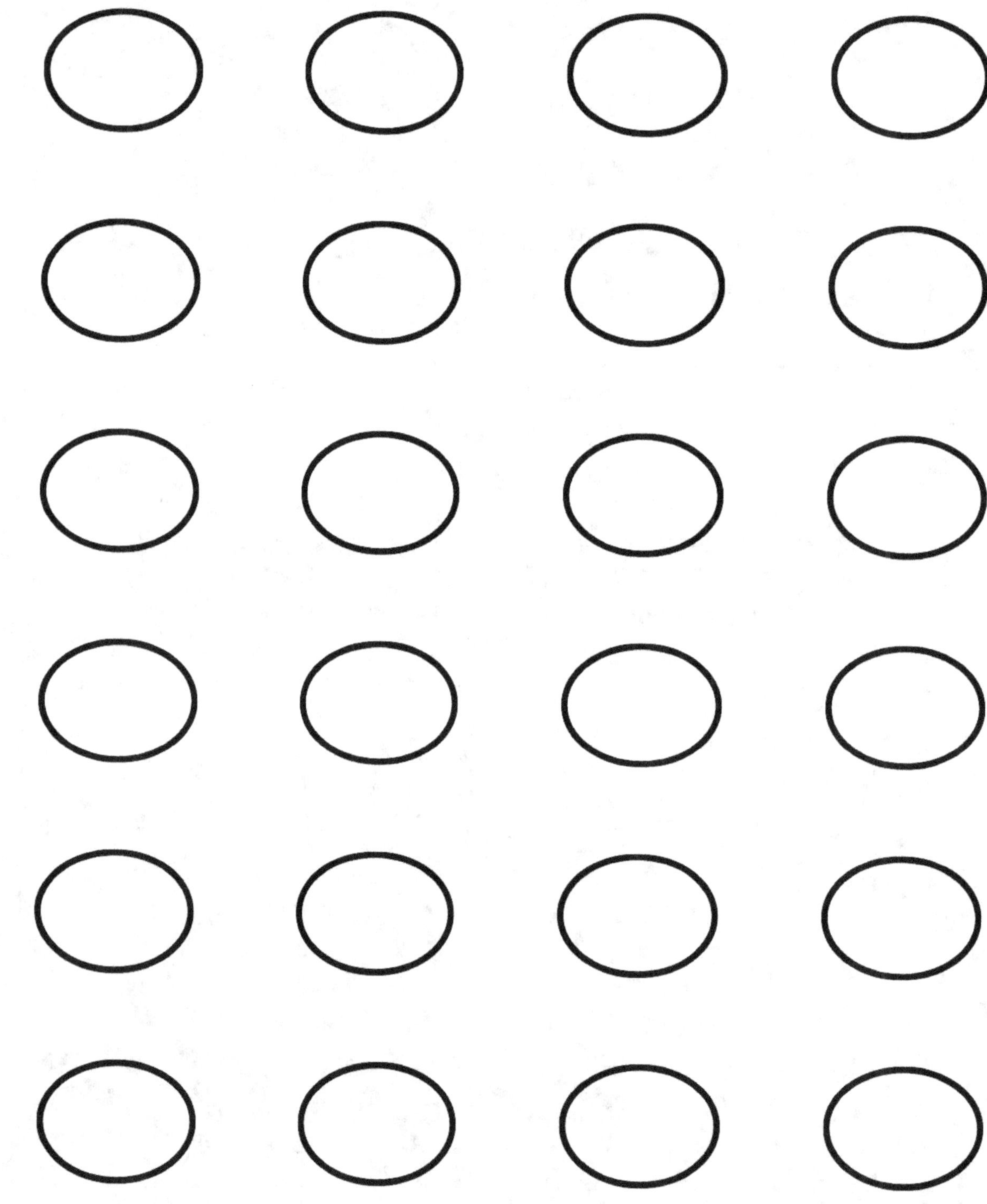

Test Color

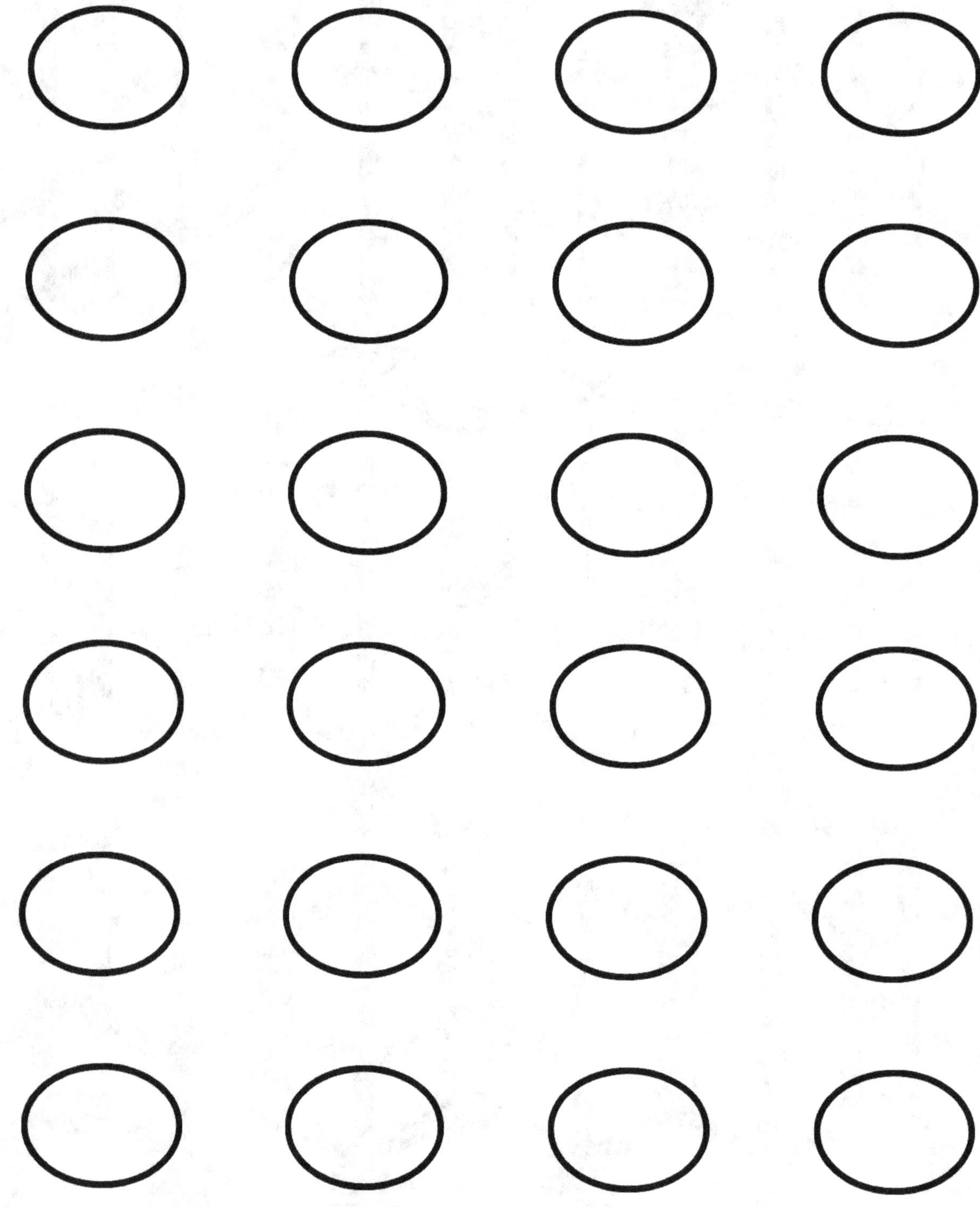

Test Color

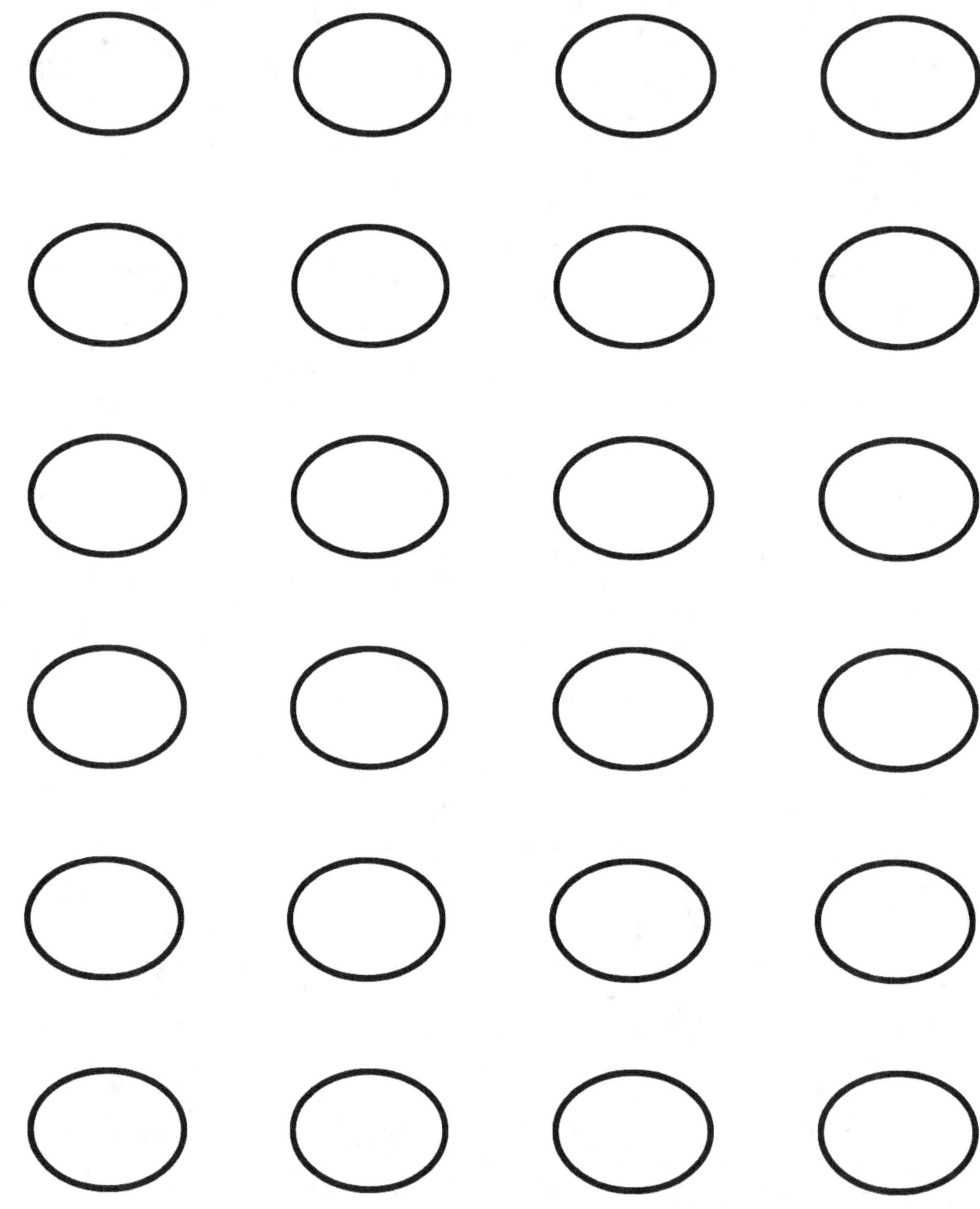

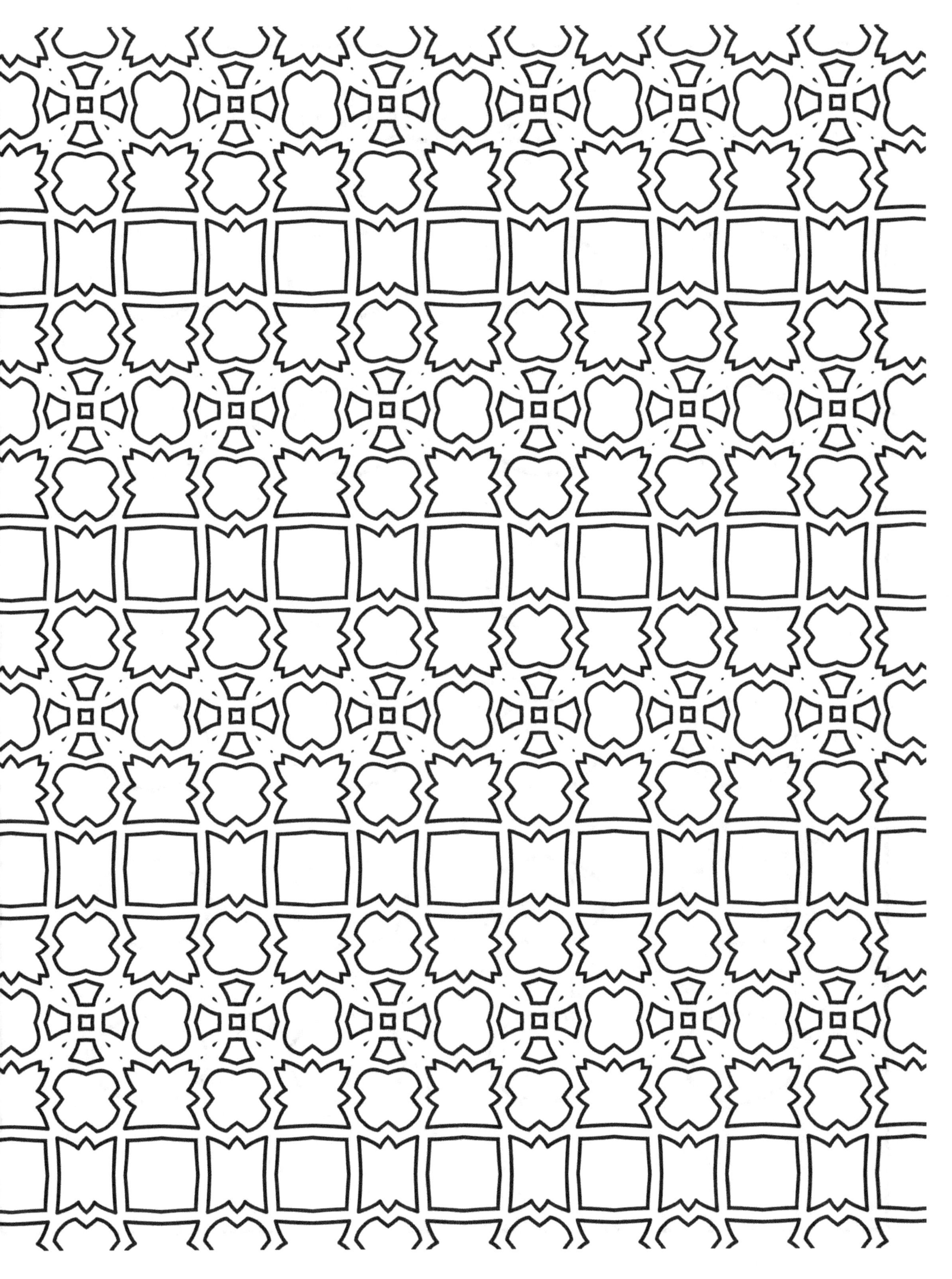

Test Color

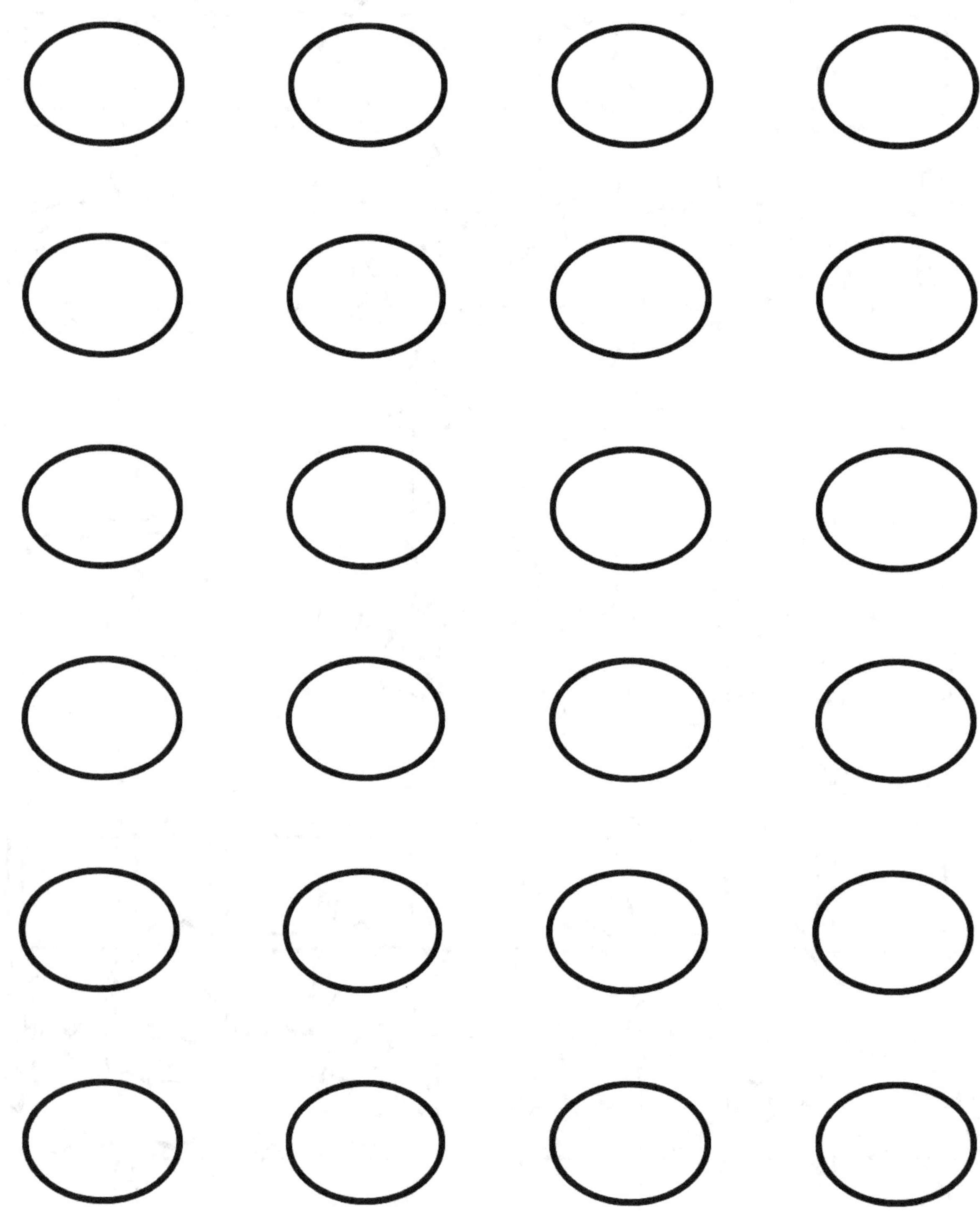

Test Color

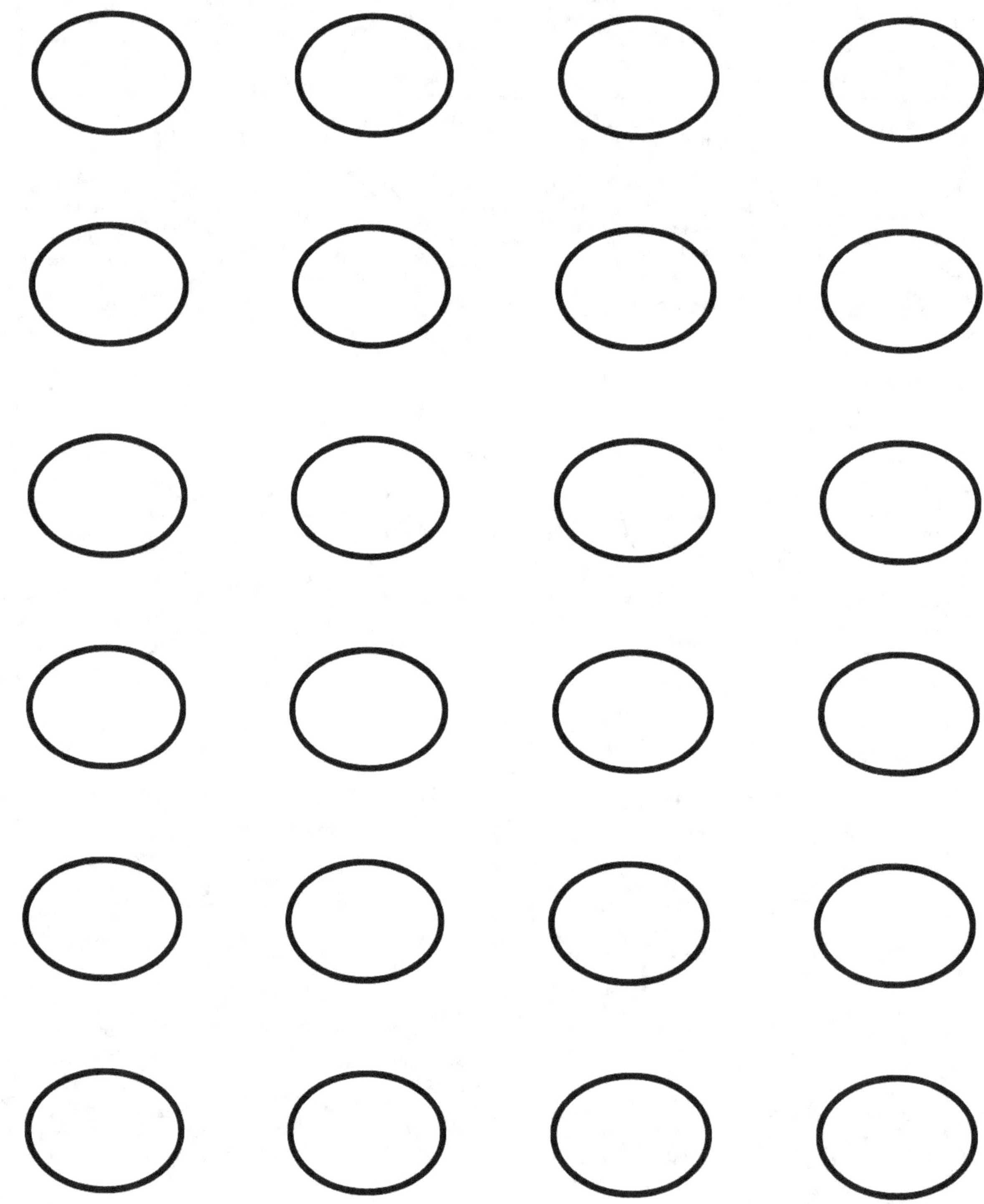

Test Color

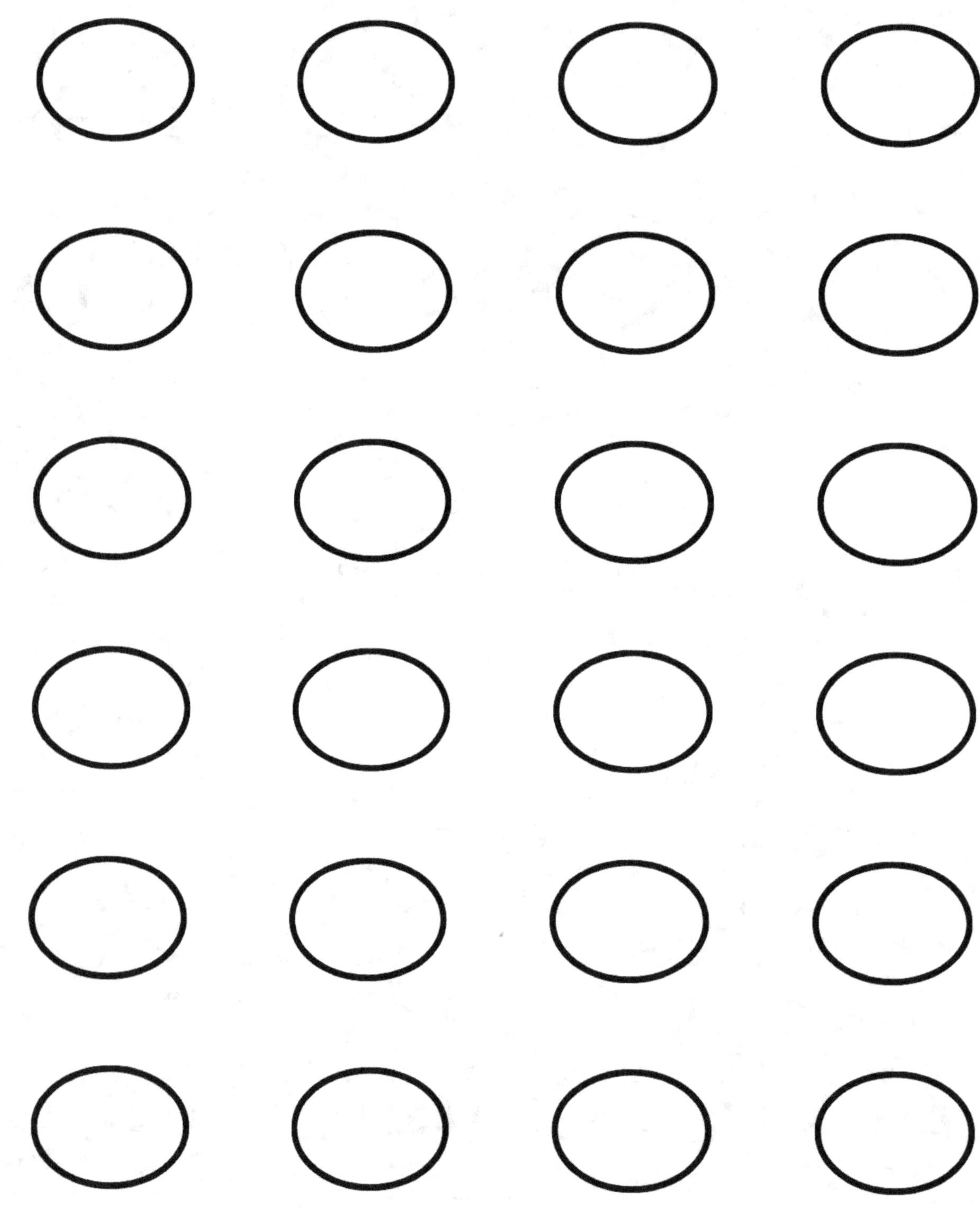

Test Color

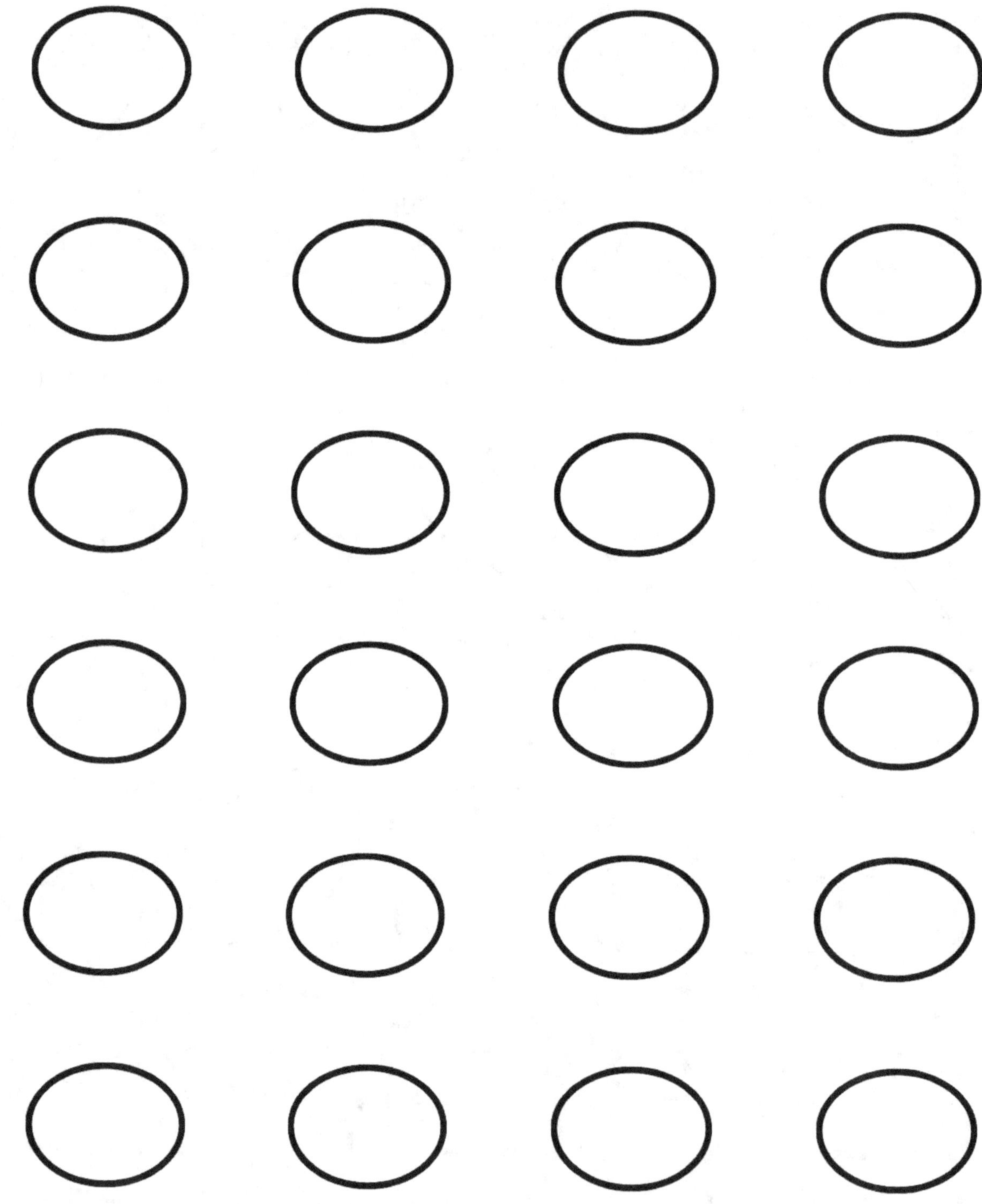

Test Color

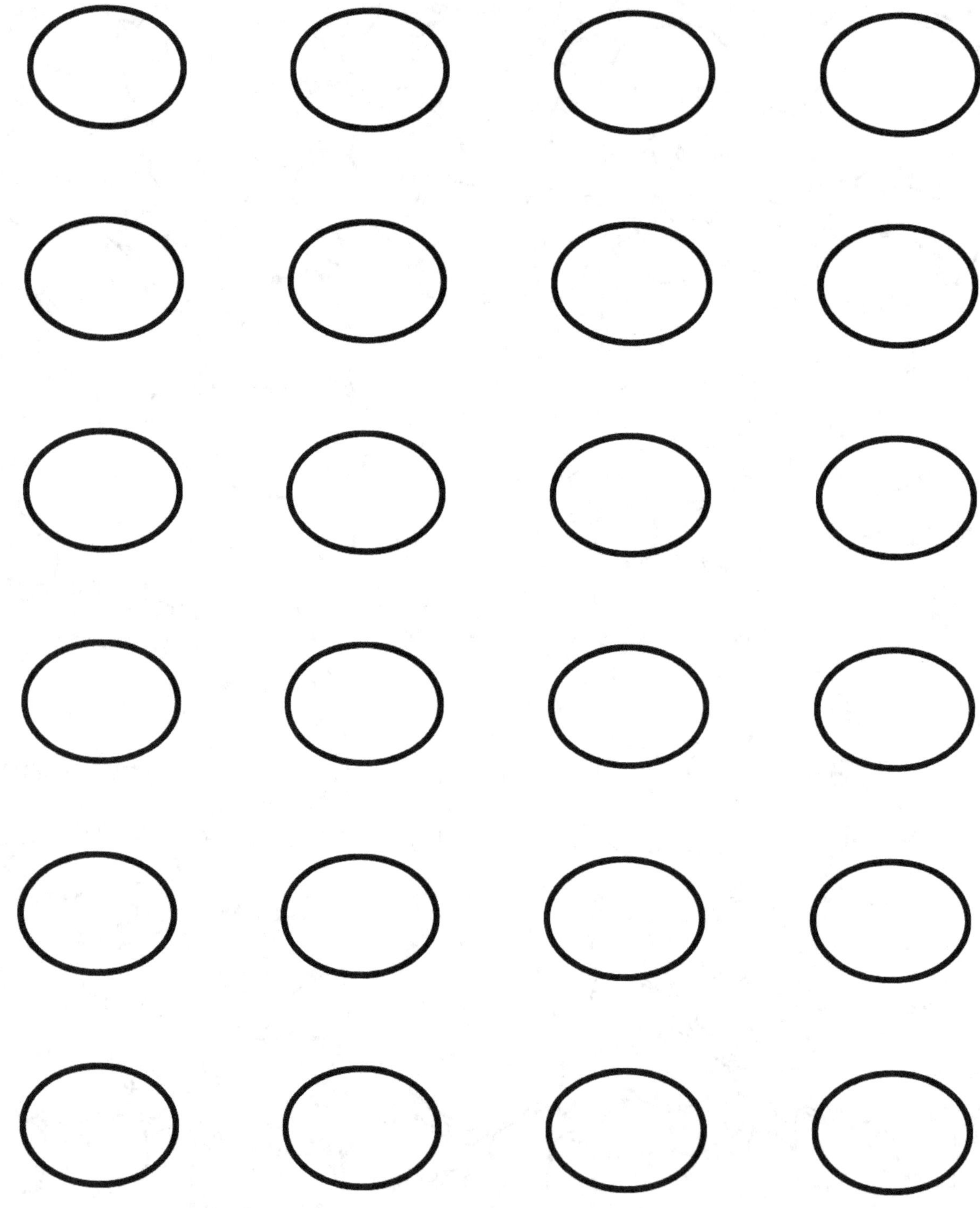

Test Color

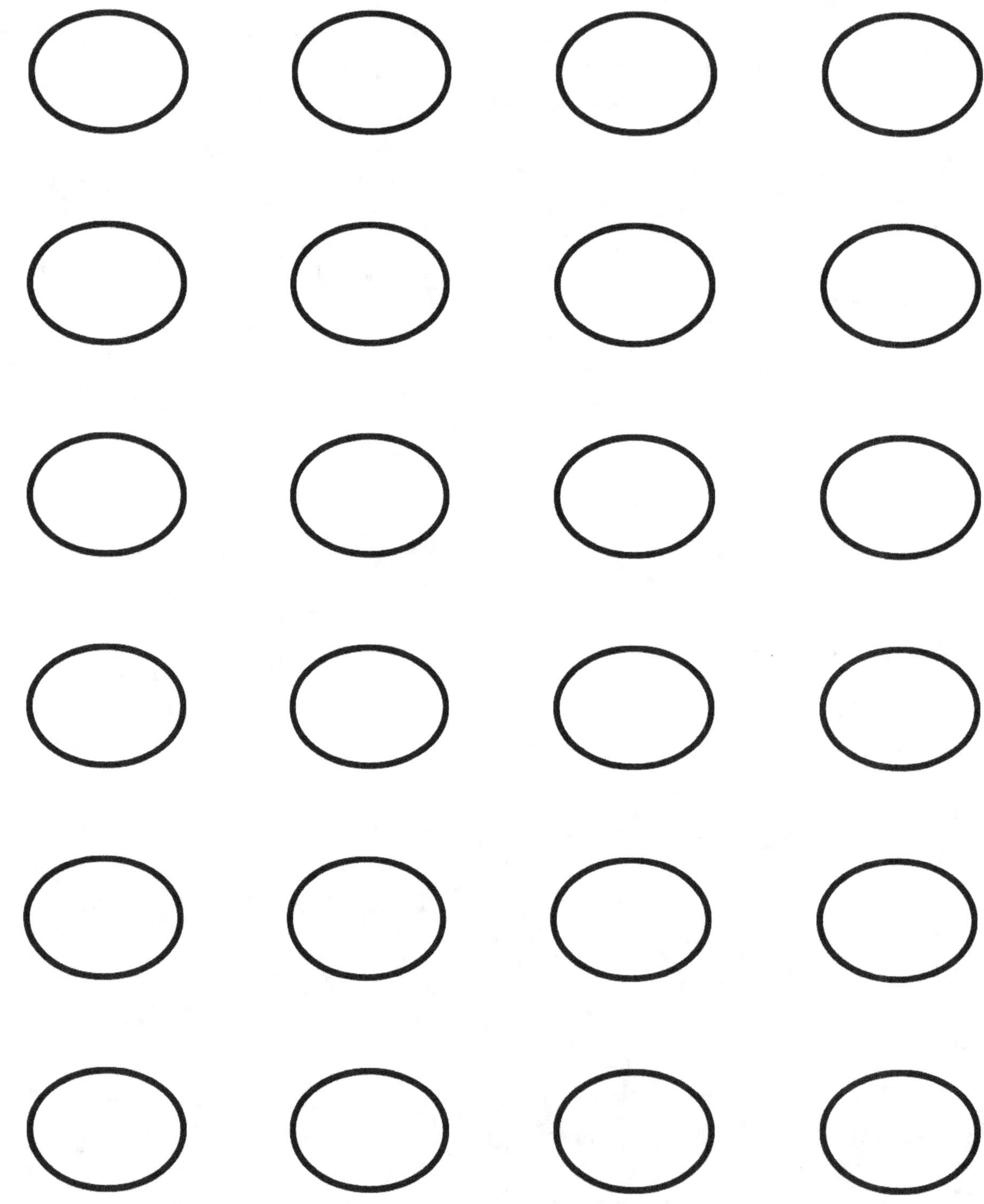

Test Color

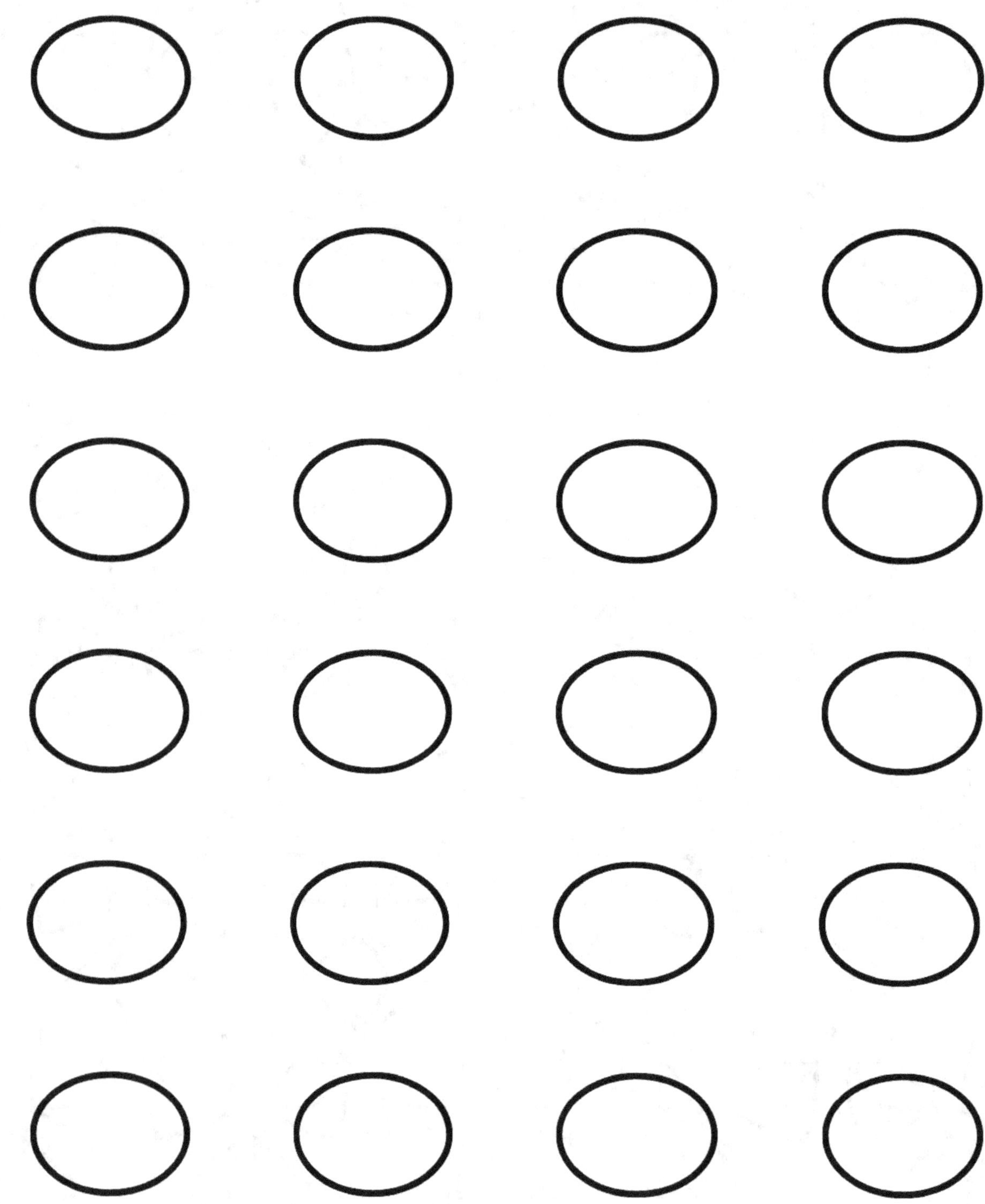

Test Color

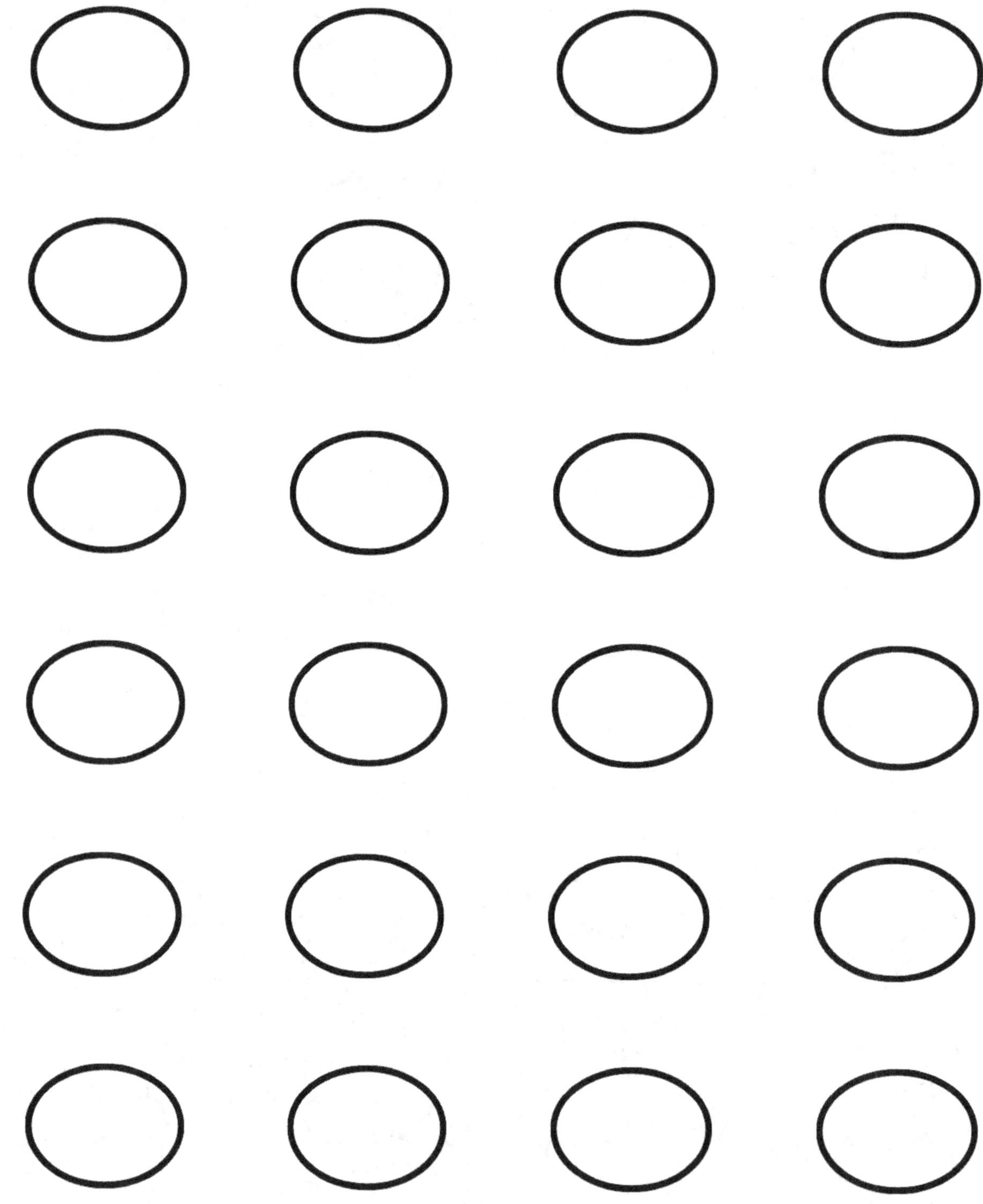

Test Color

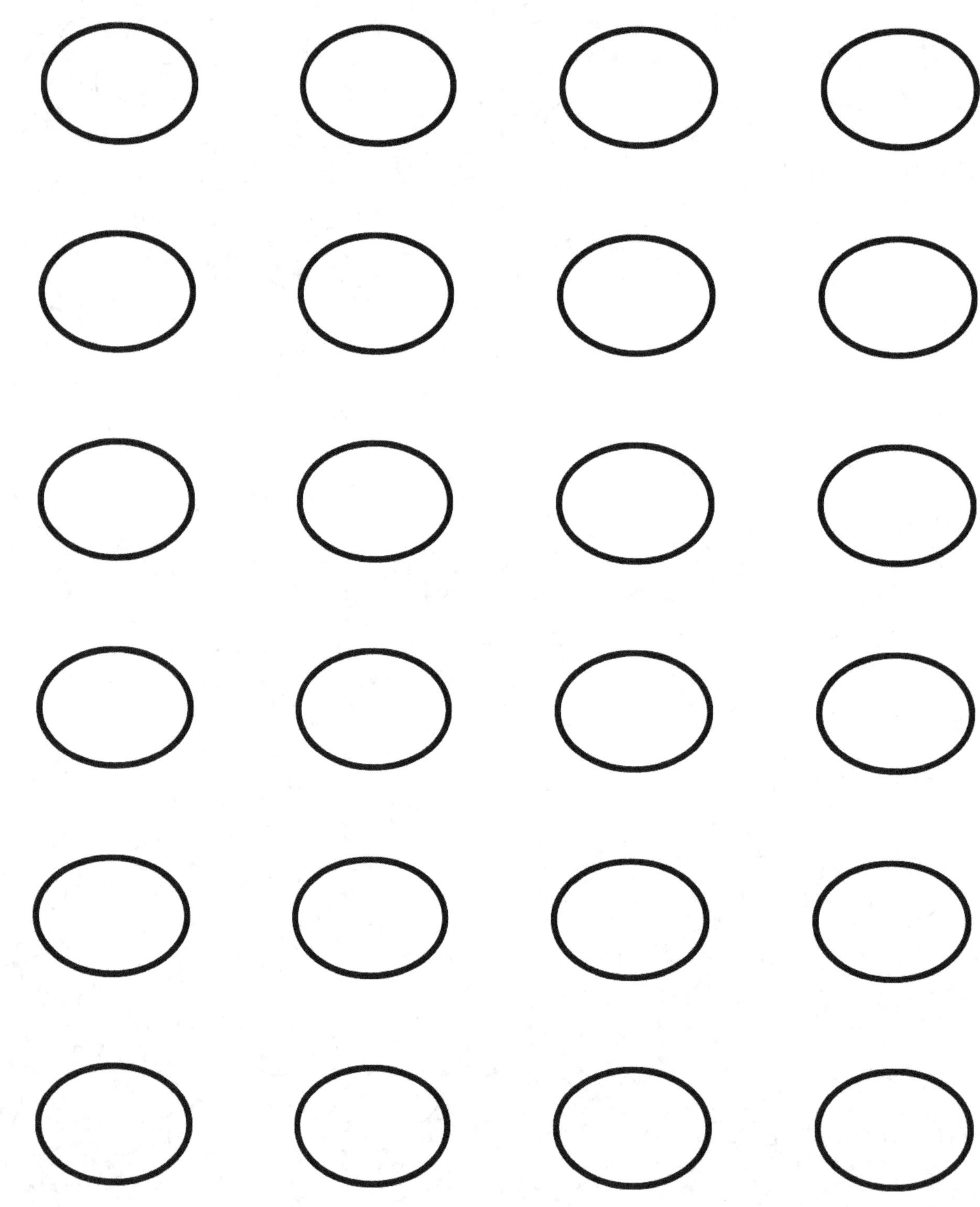

Test Color

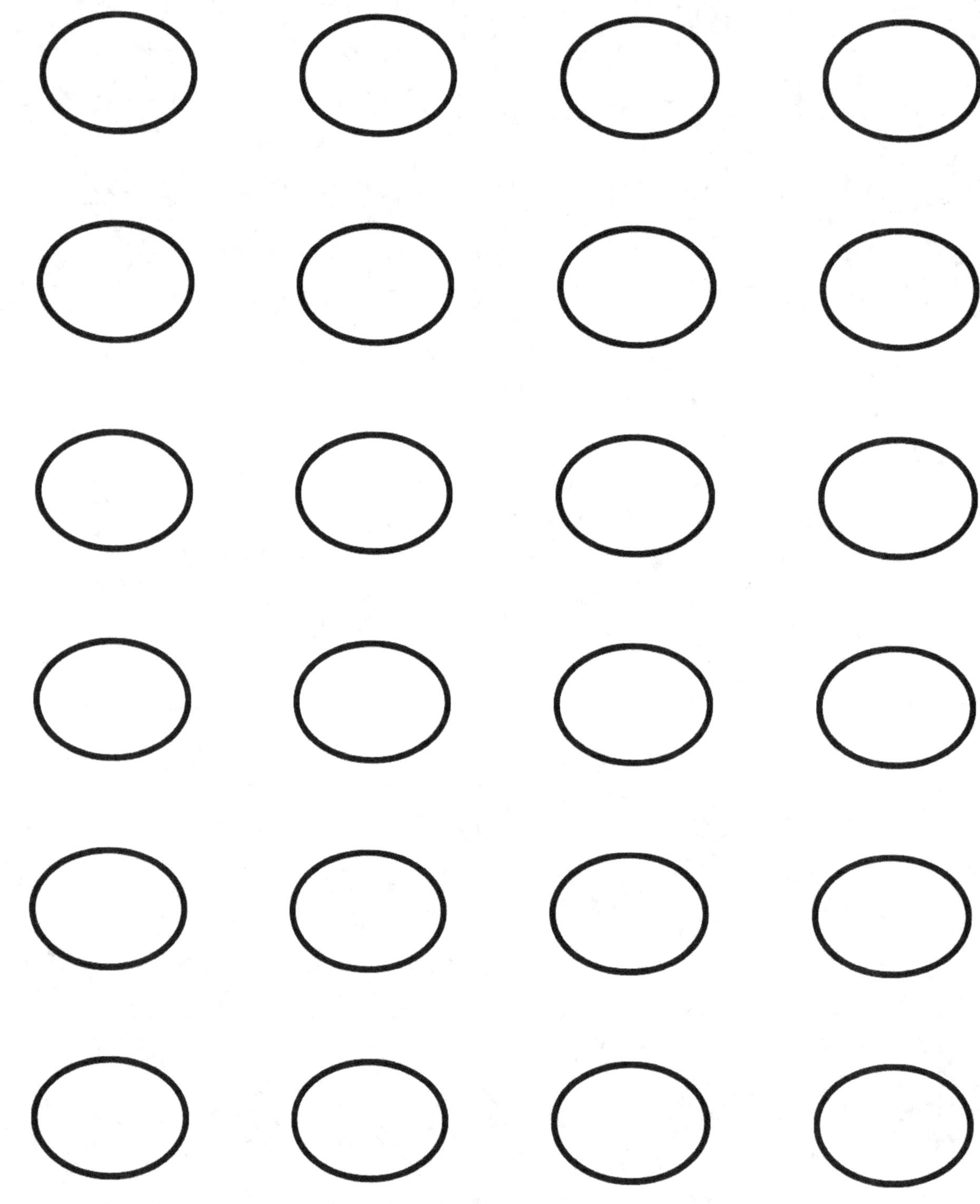

Test Color

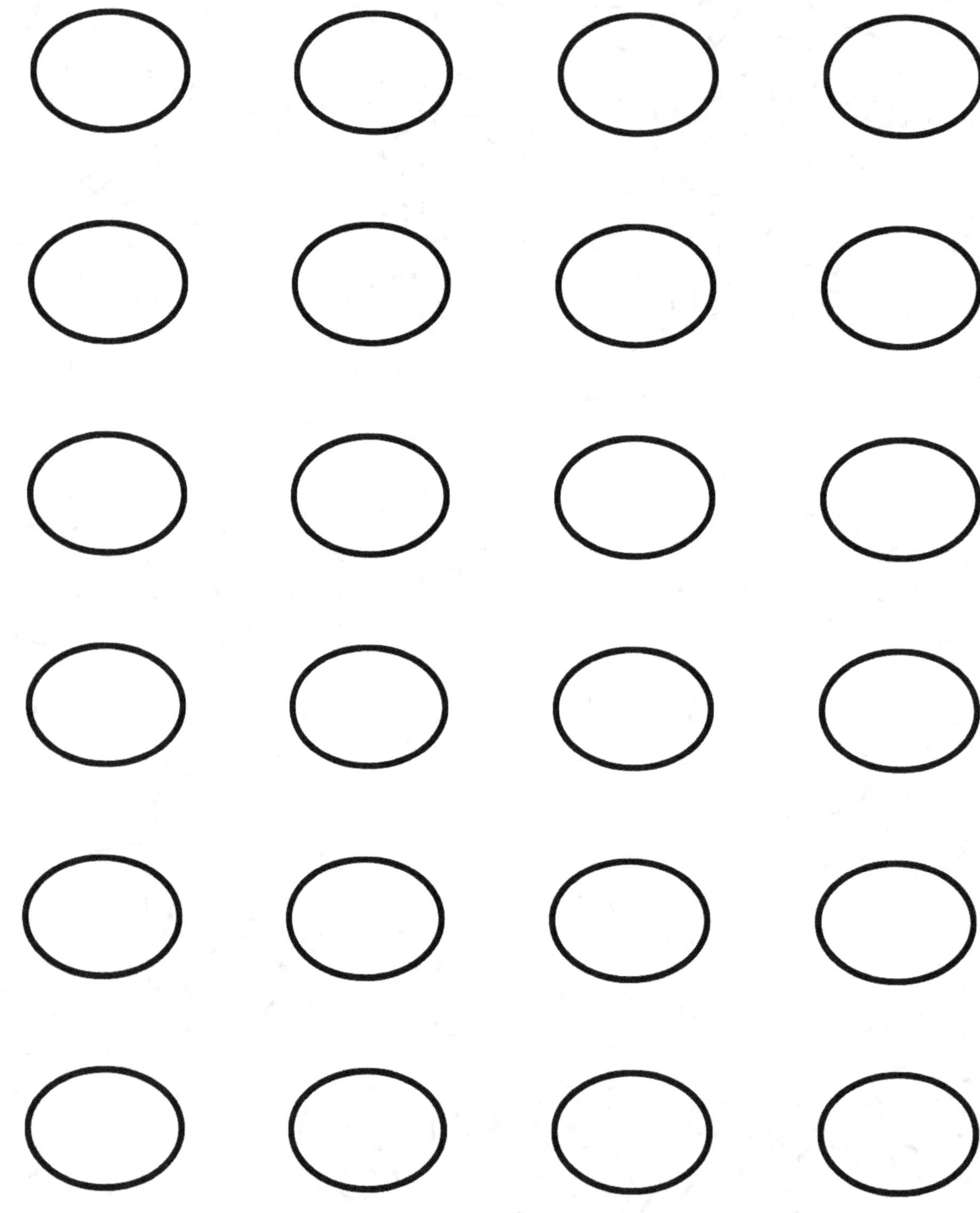

Test Color

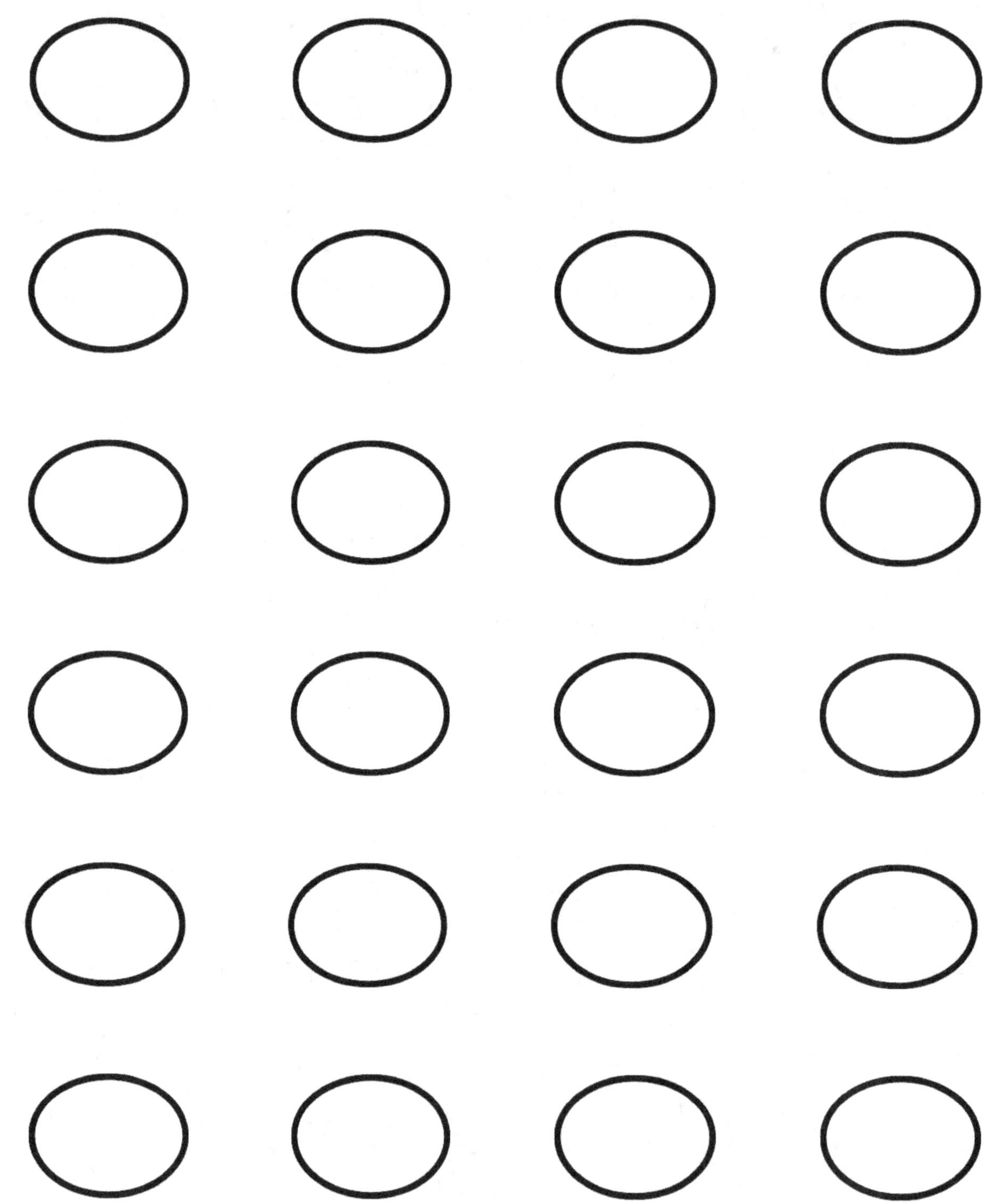

Test Color

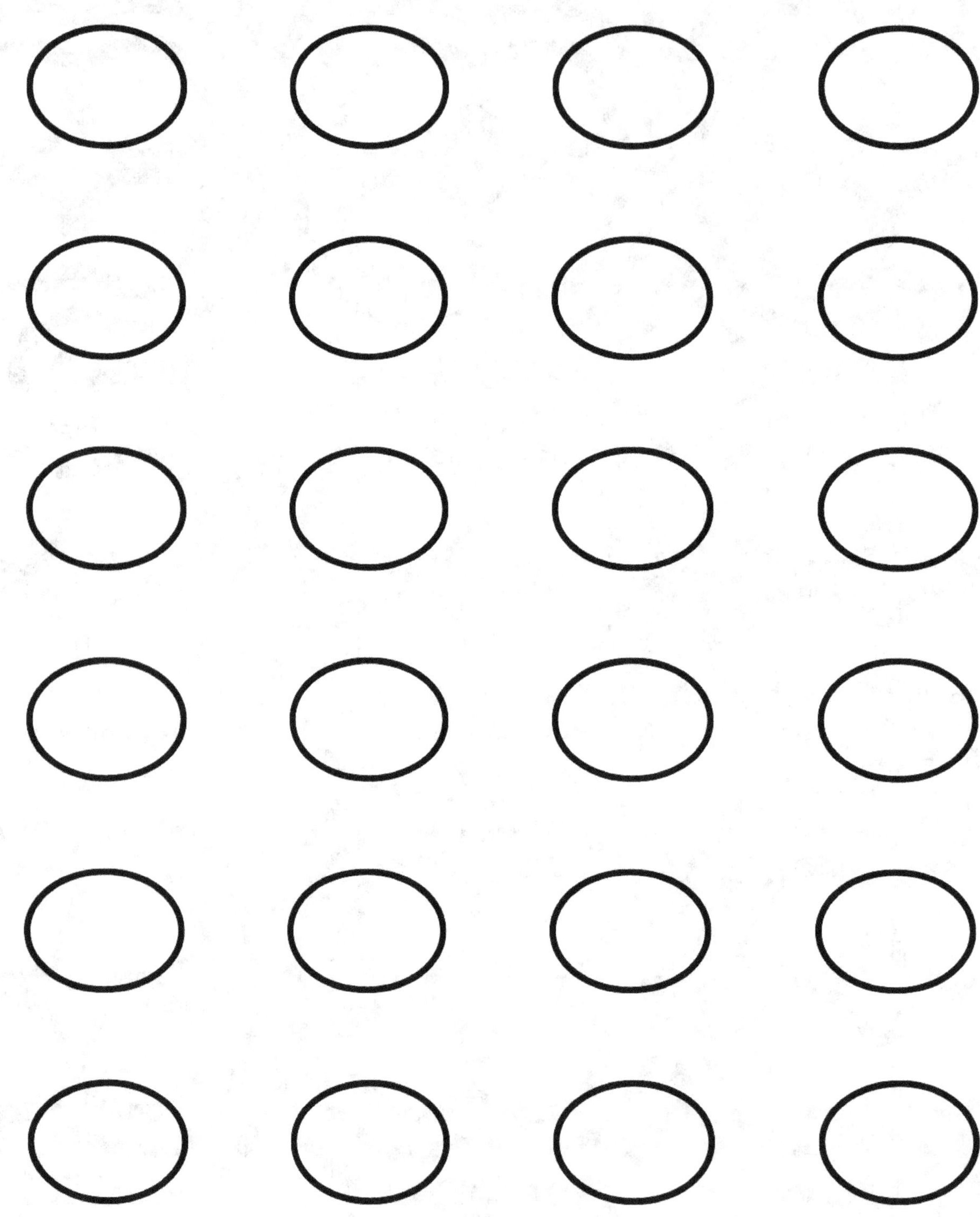

Test Color

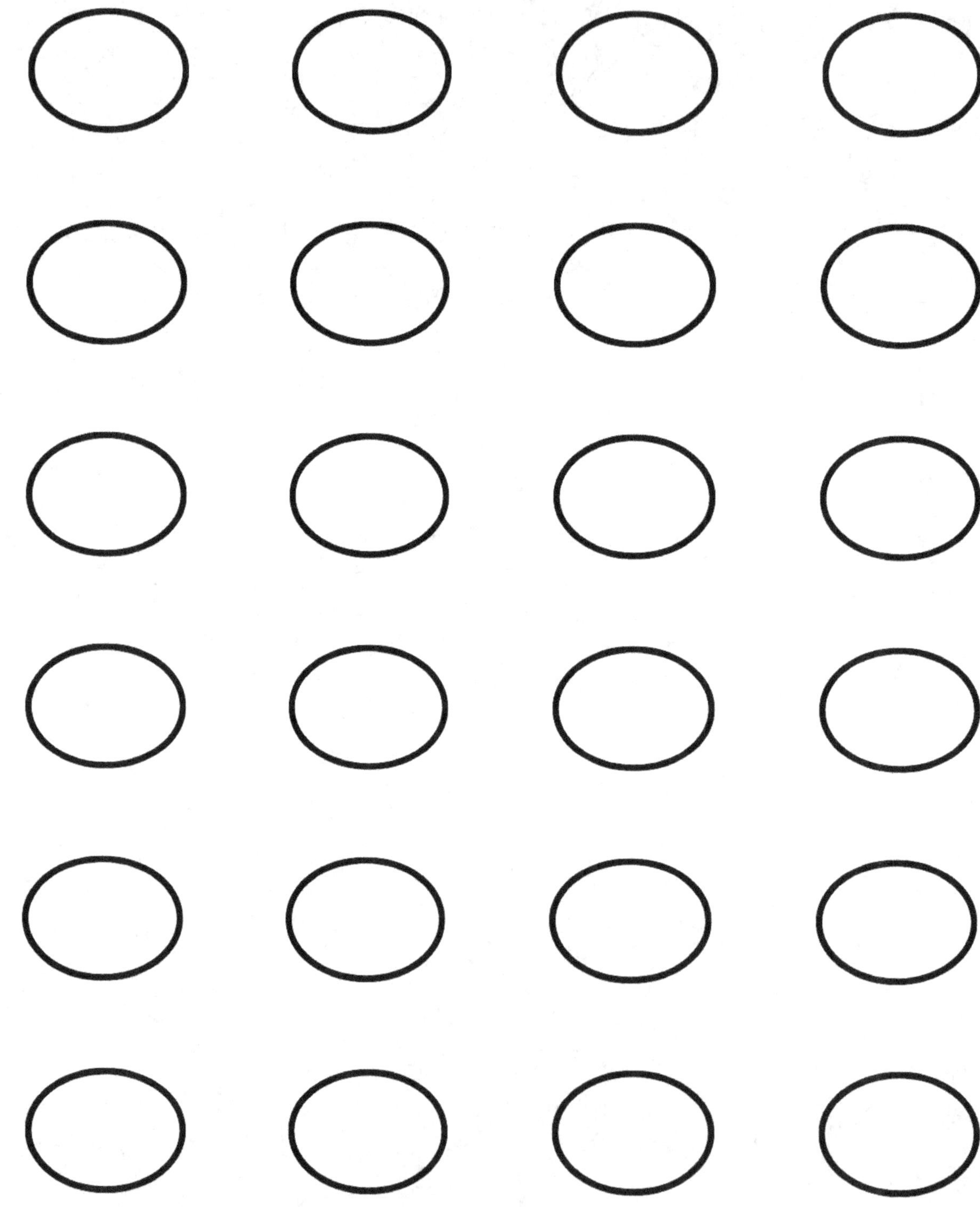

Test Color

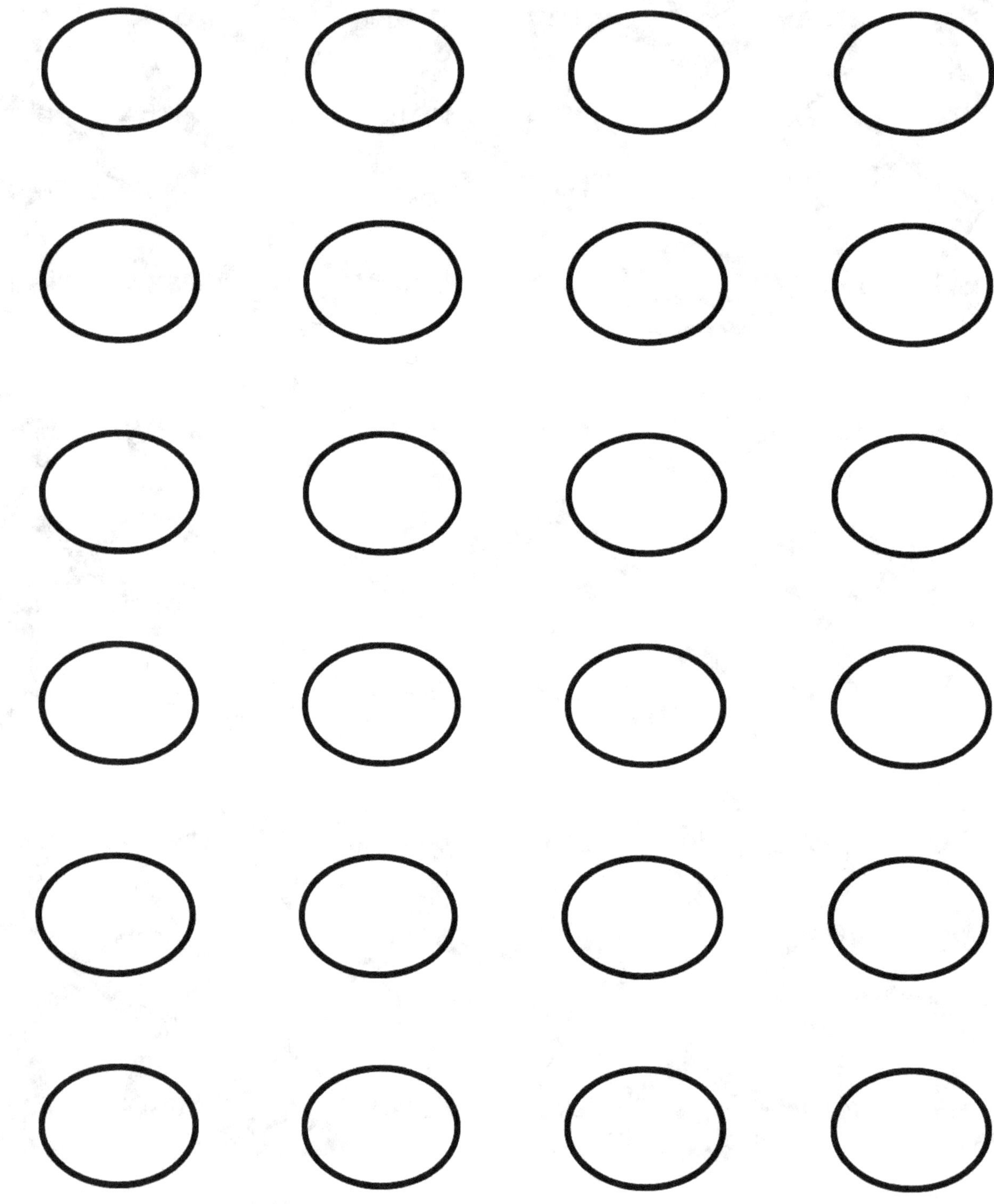

Test Color

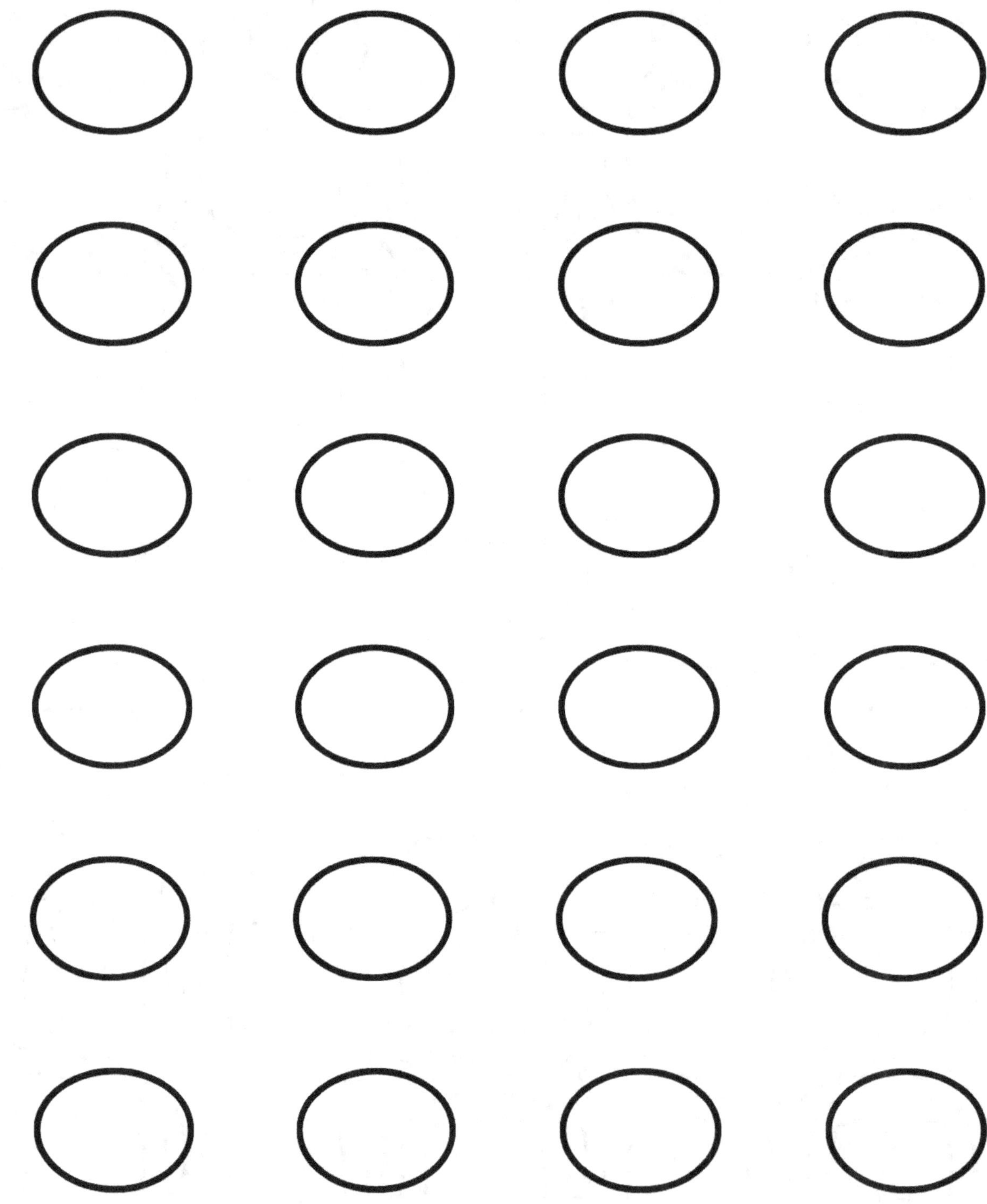

Test Color

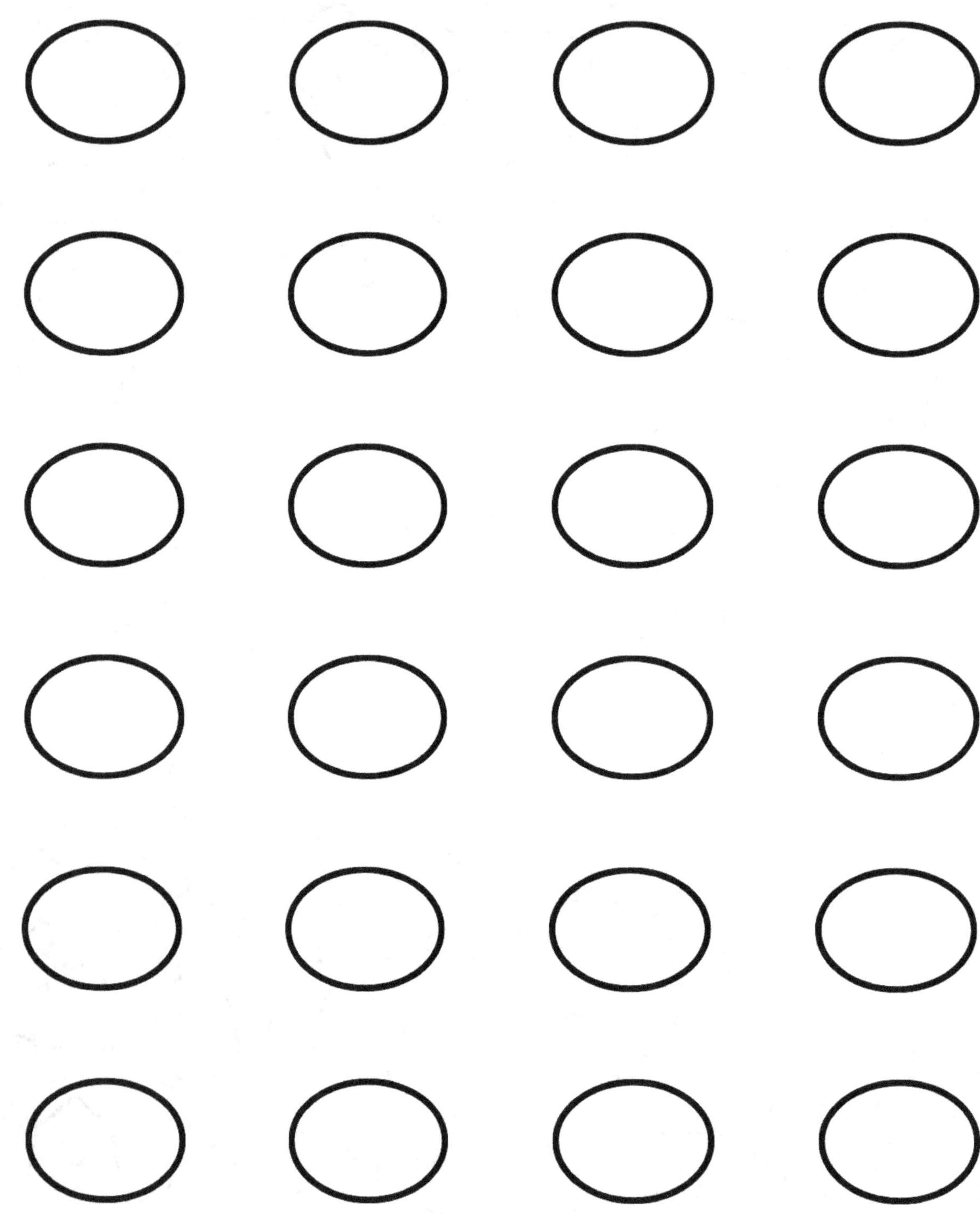

Test Color

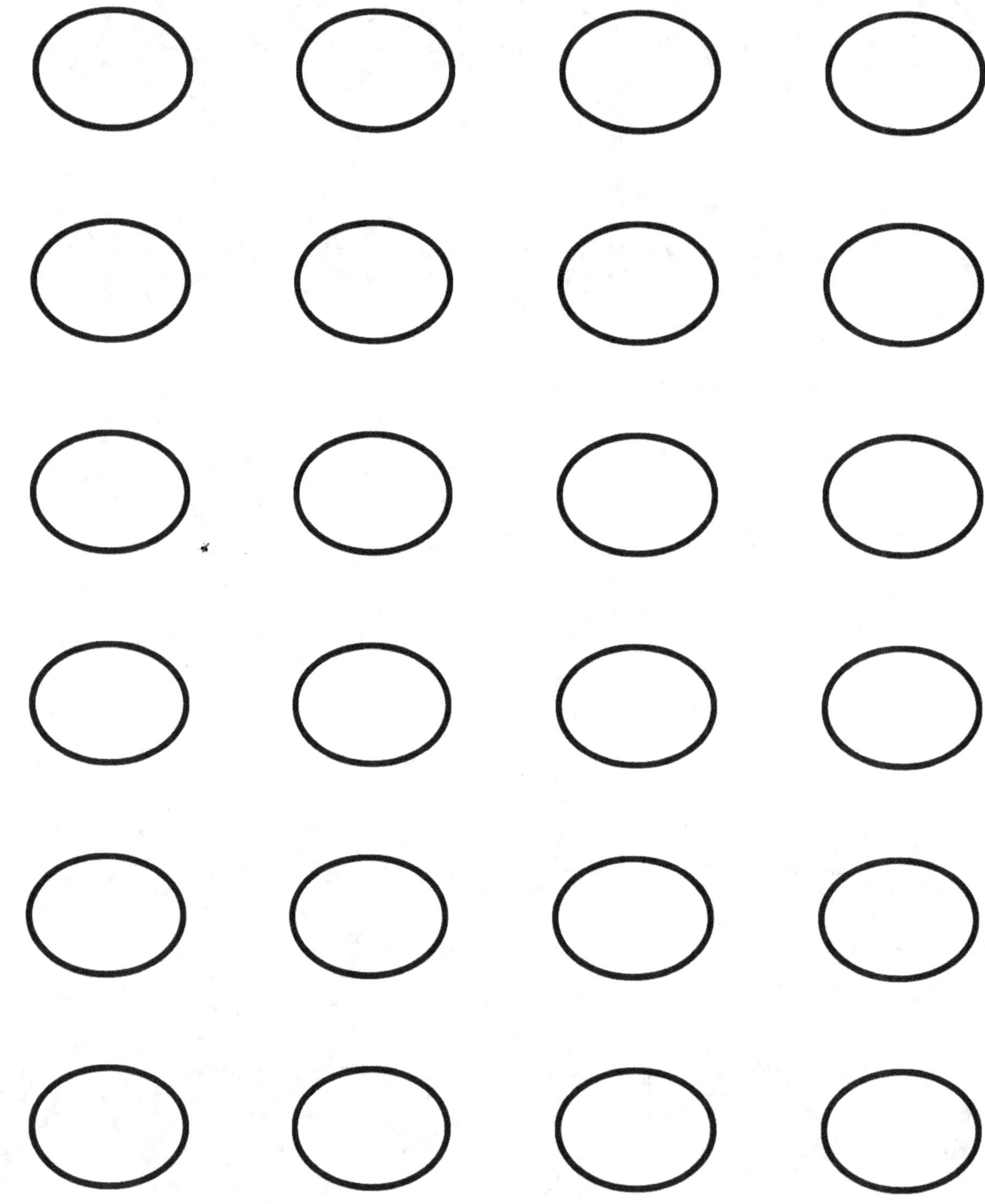

Test Color

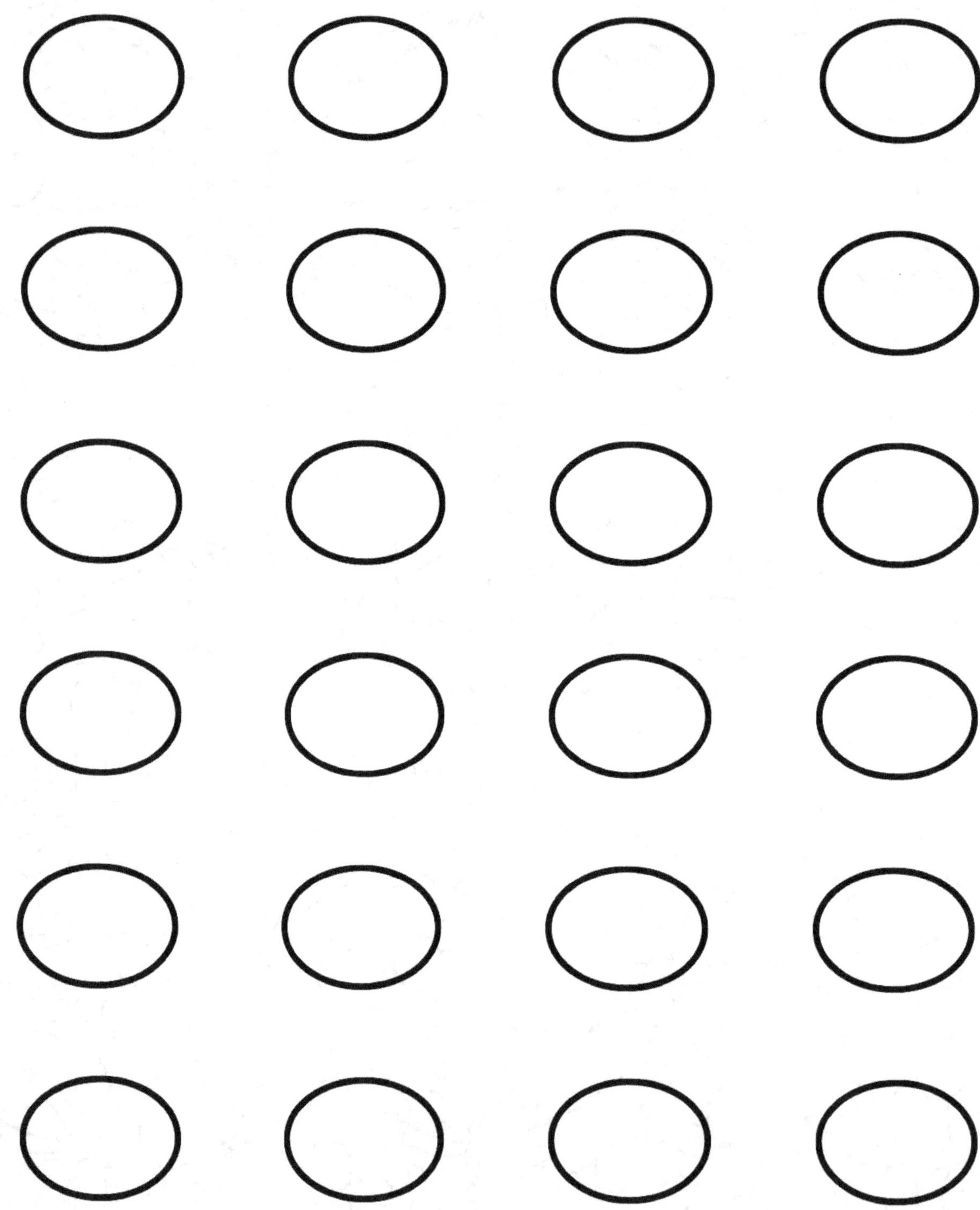

Test Color

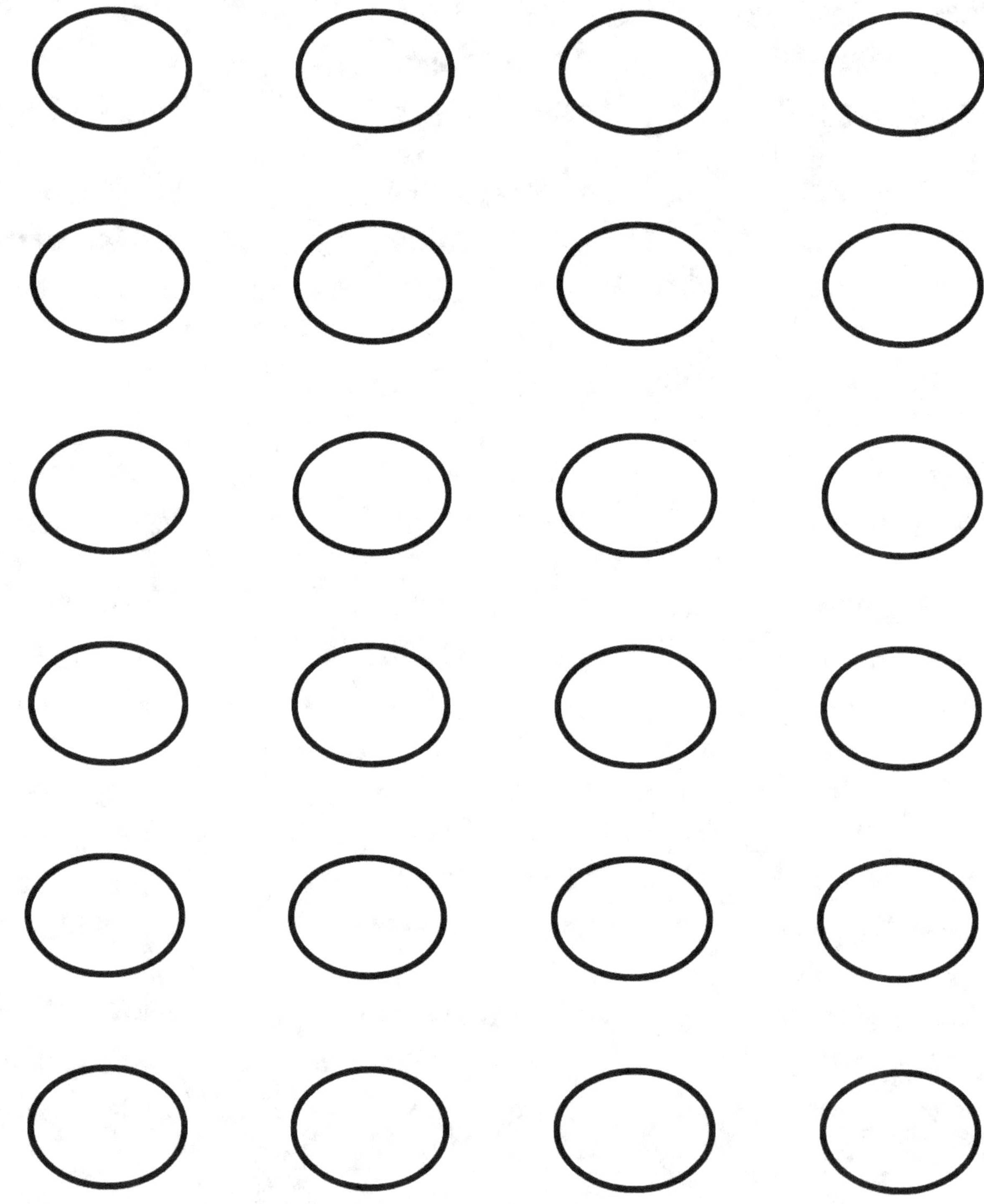

Test Color

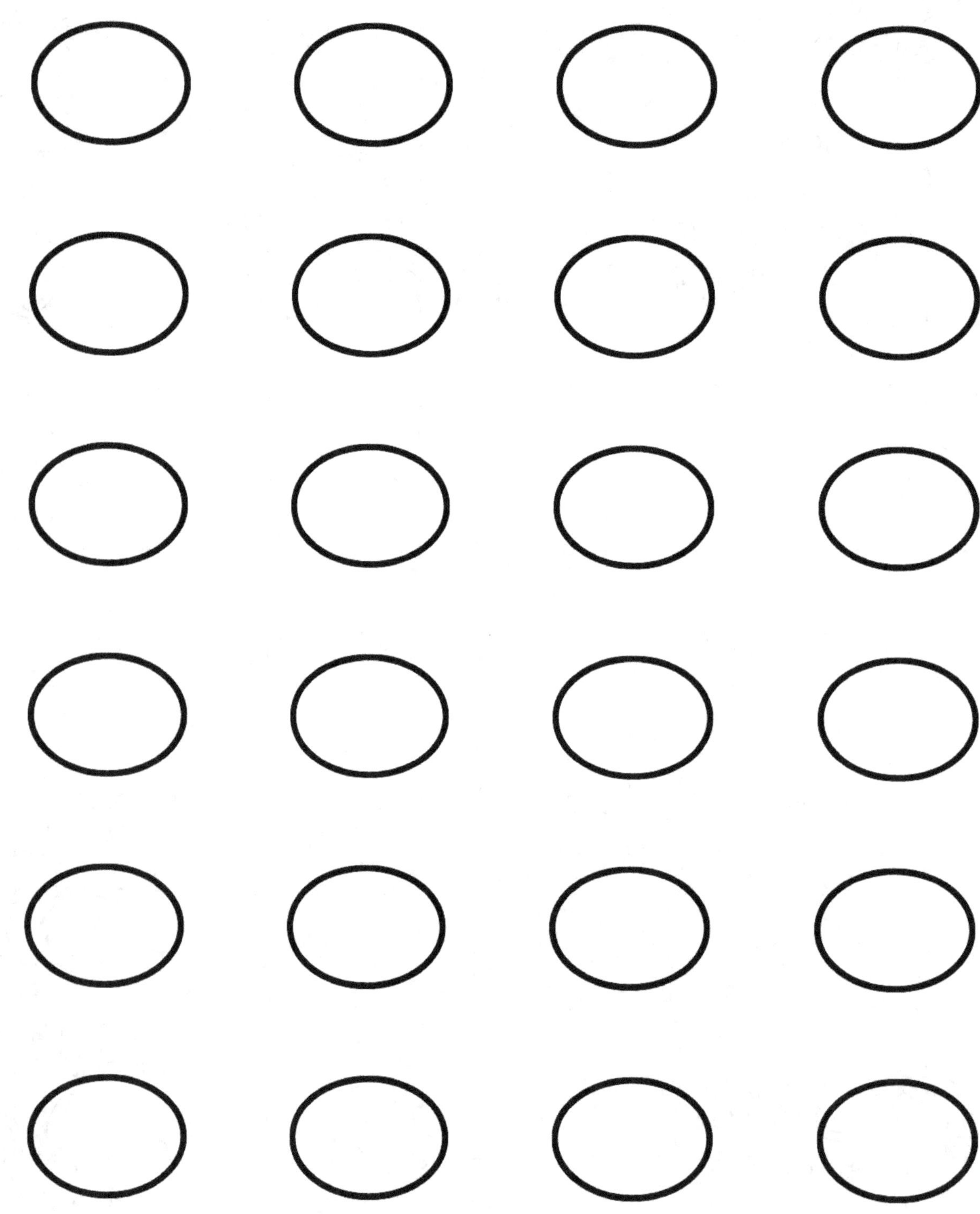

Test Color

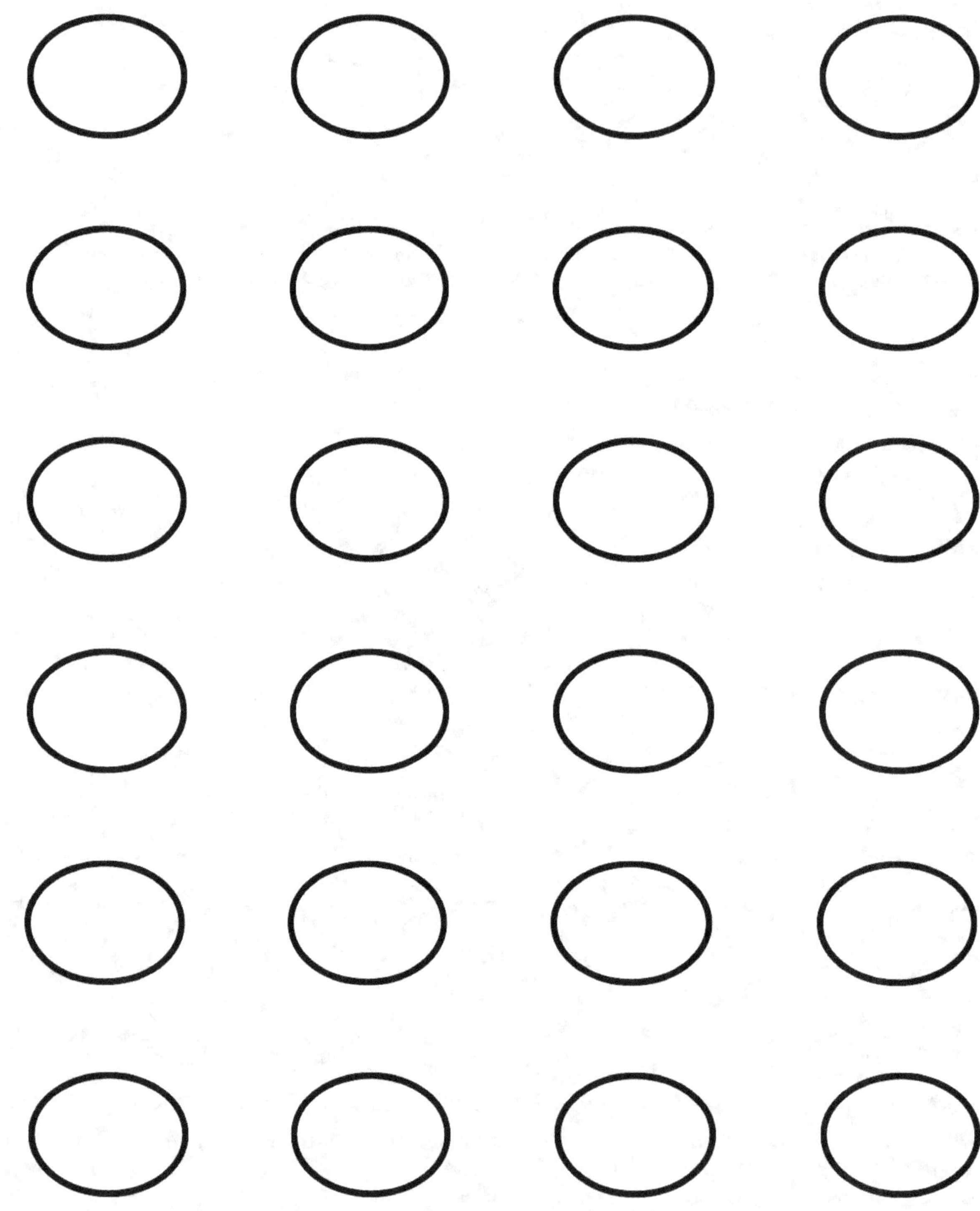

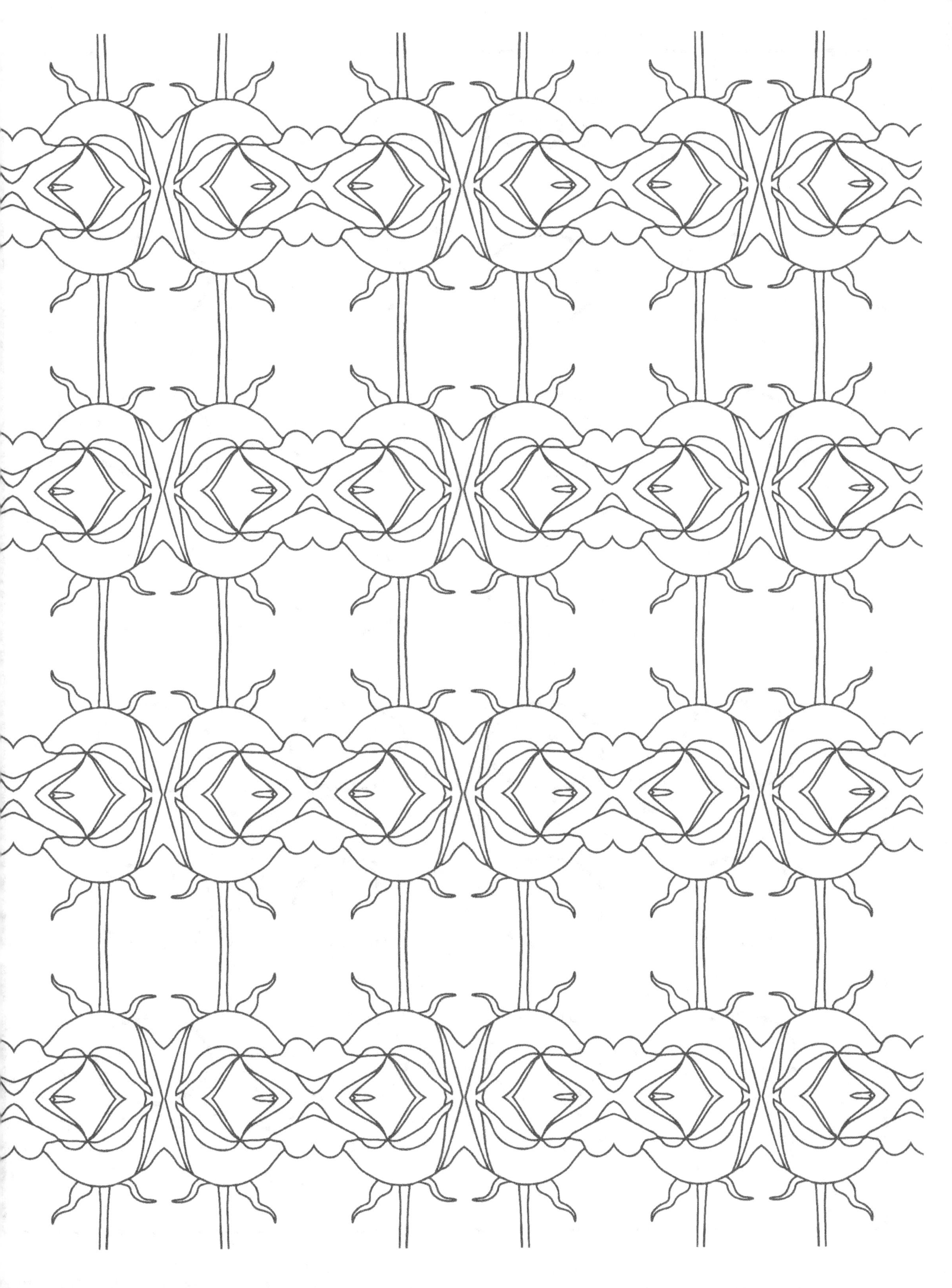

Test Color

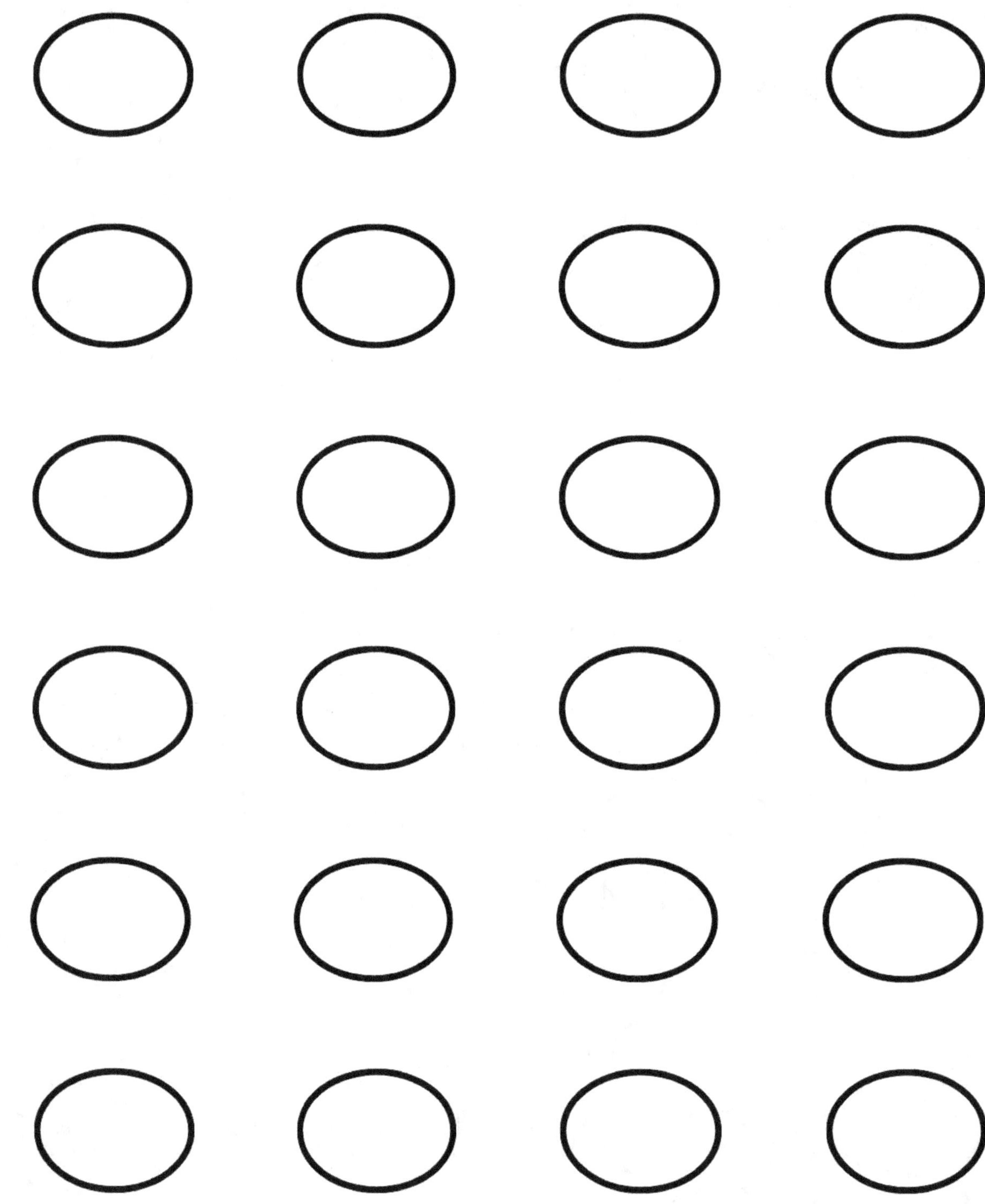

Test Color

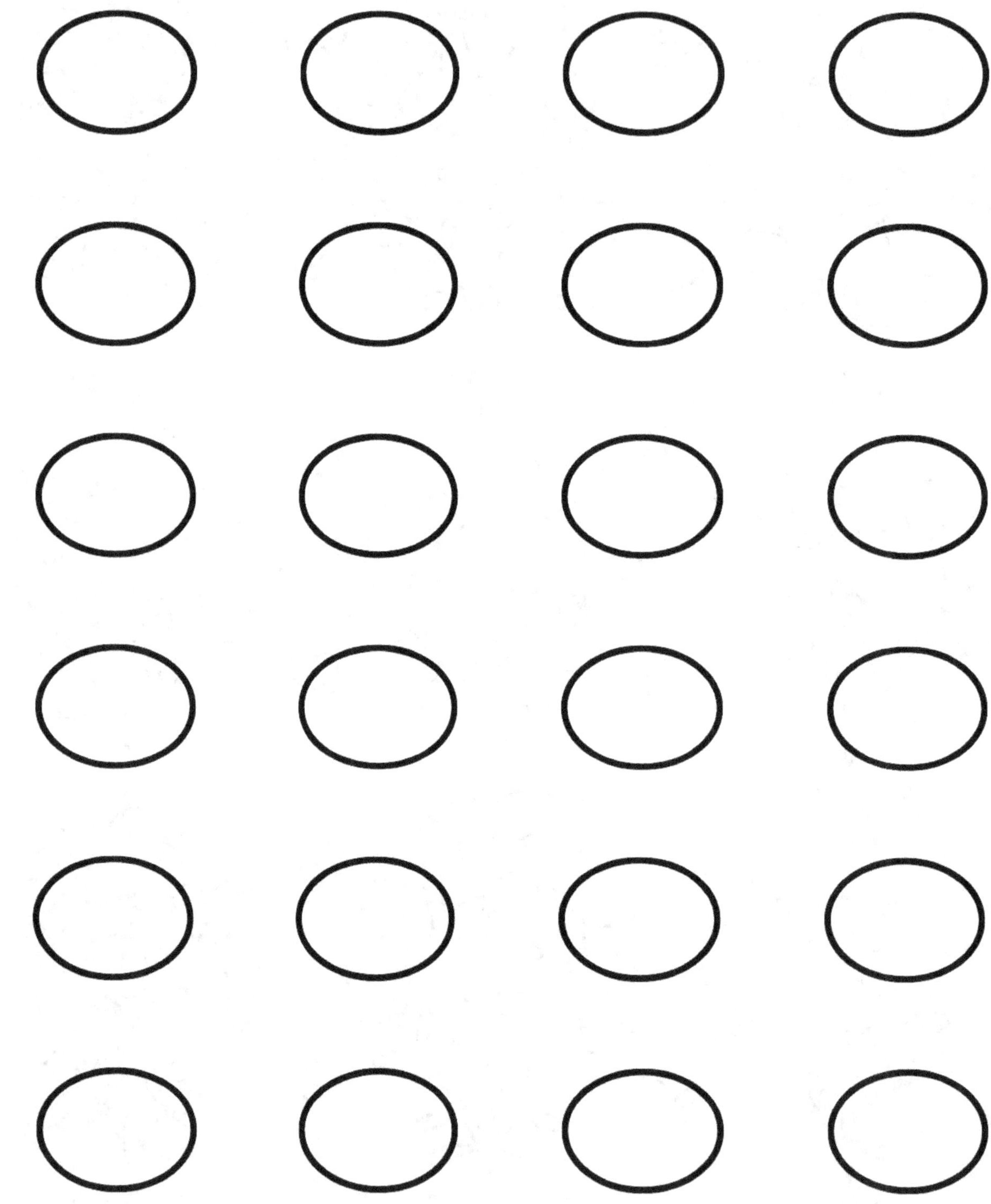

Test Color

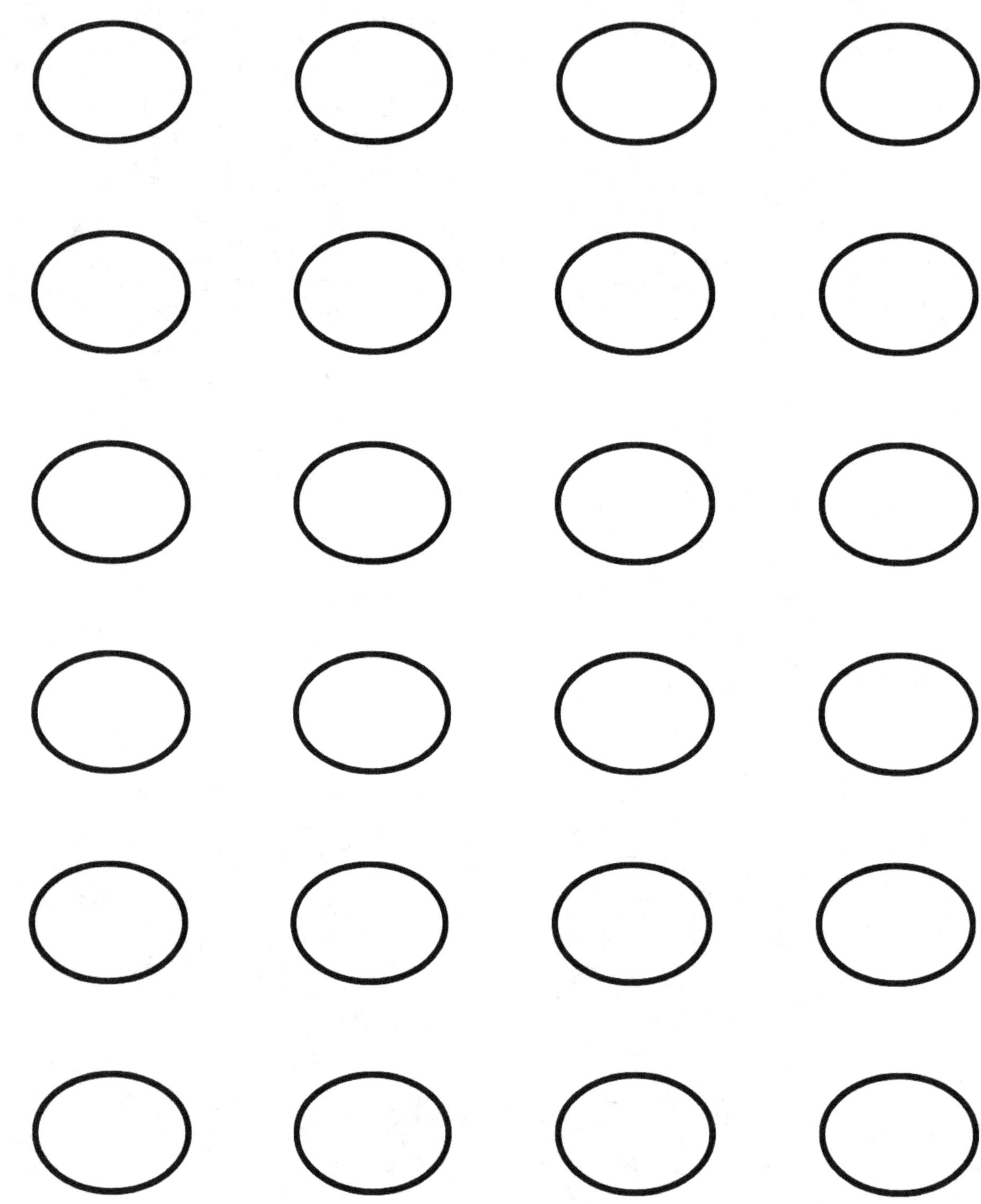

Test Color

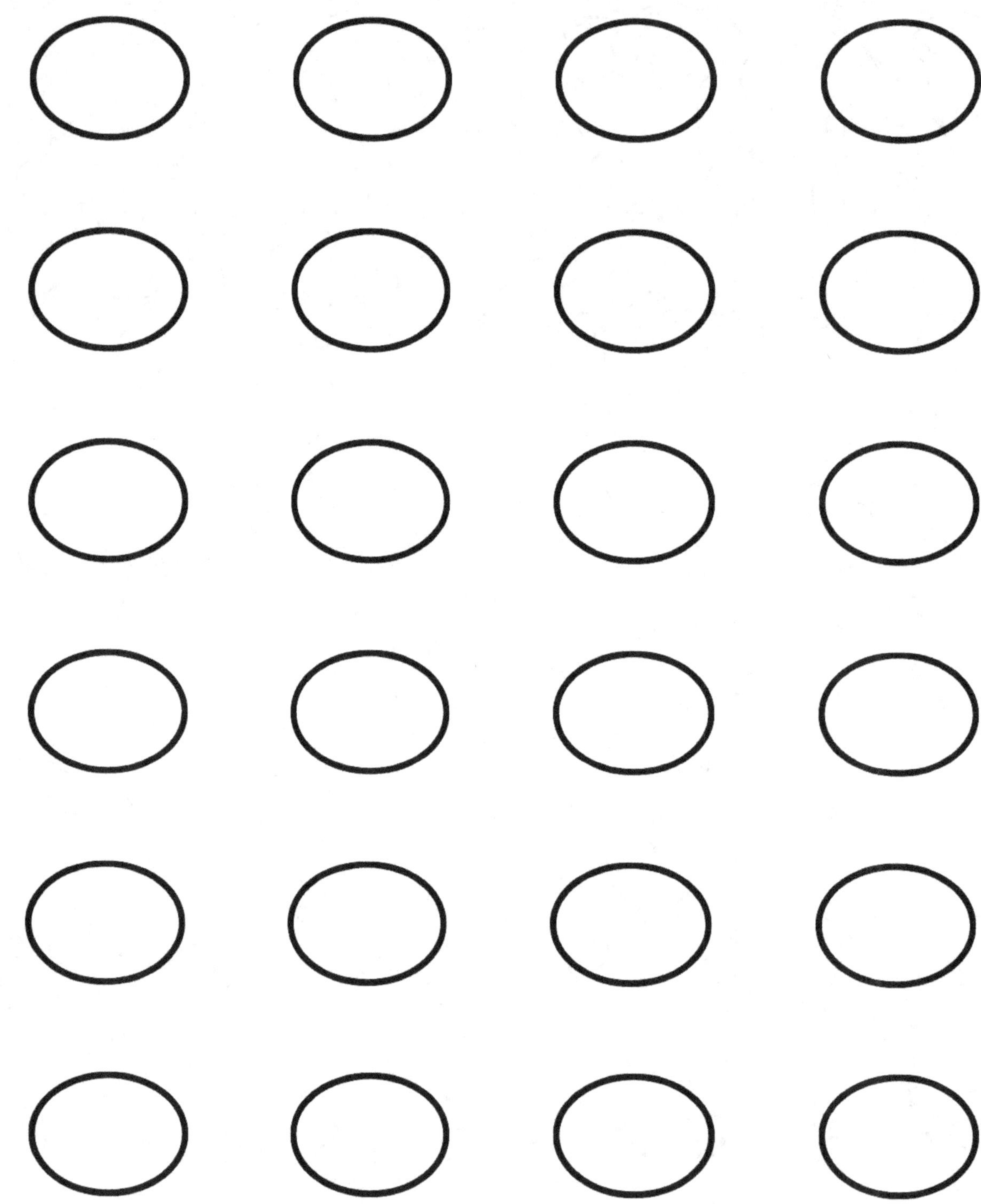

Test Color

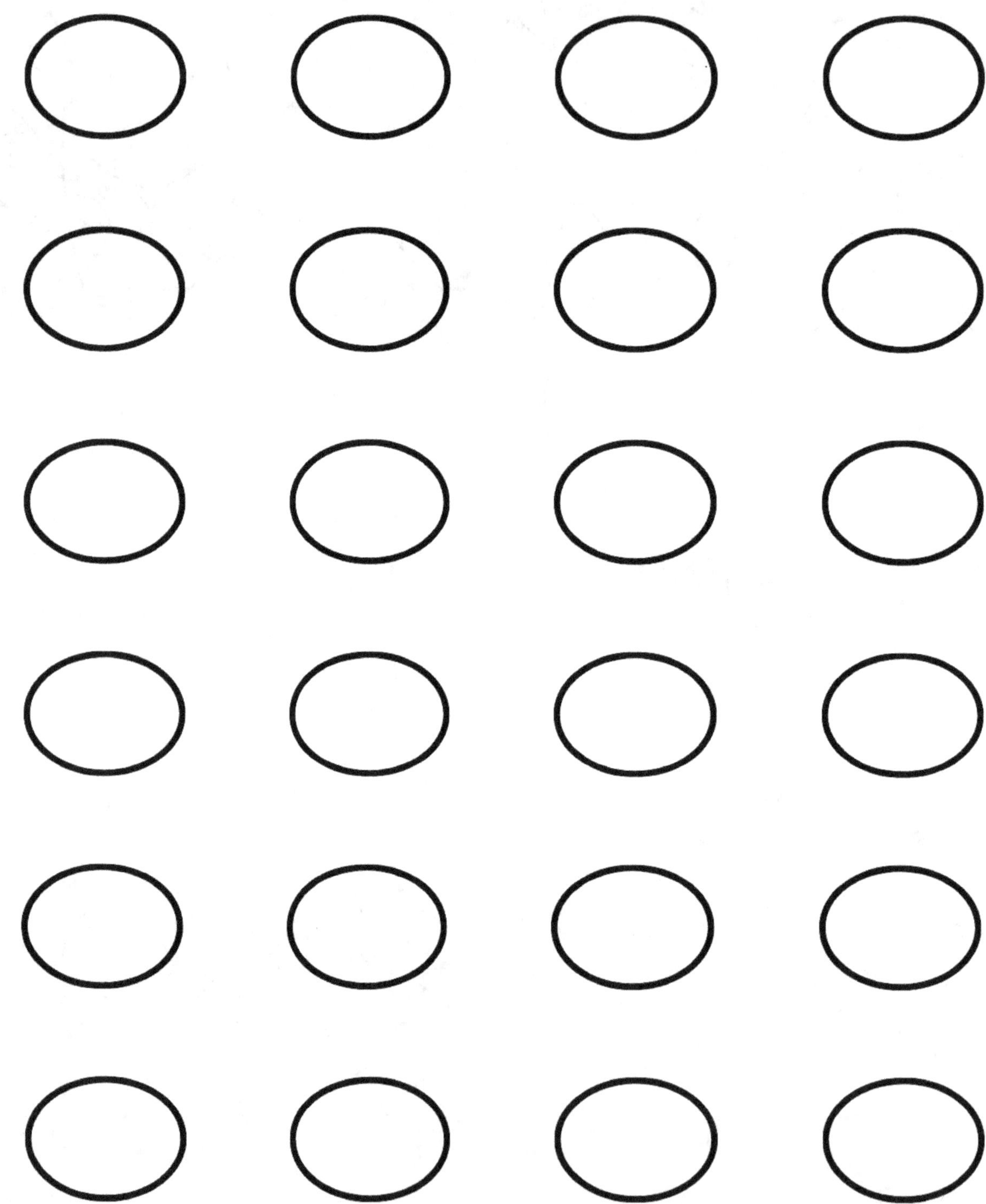

Test Color

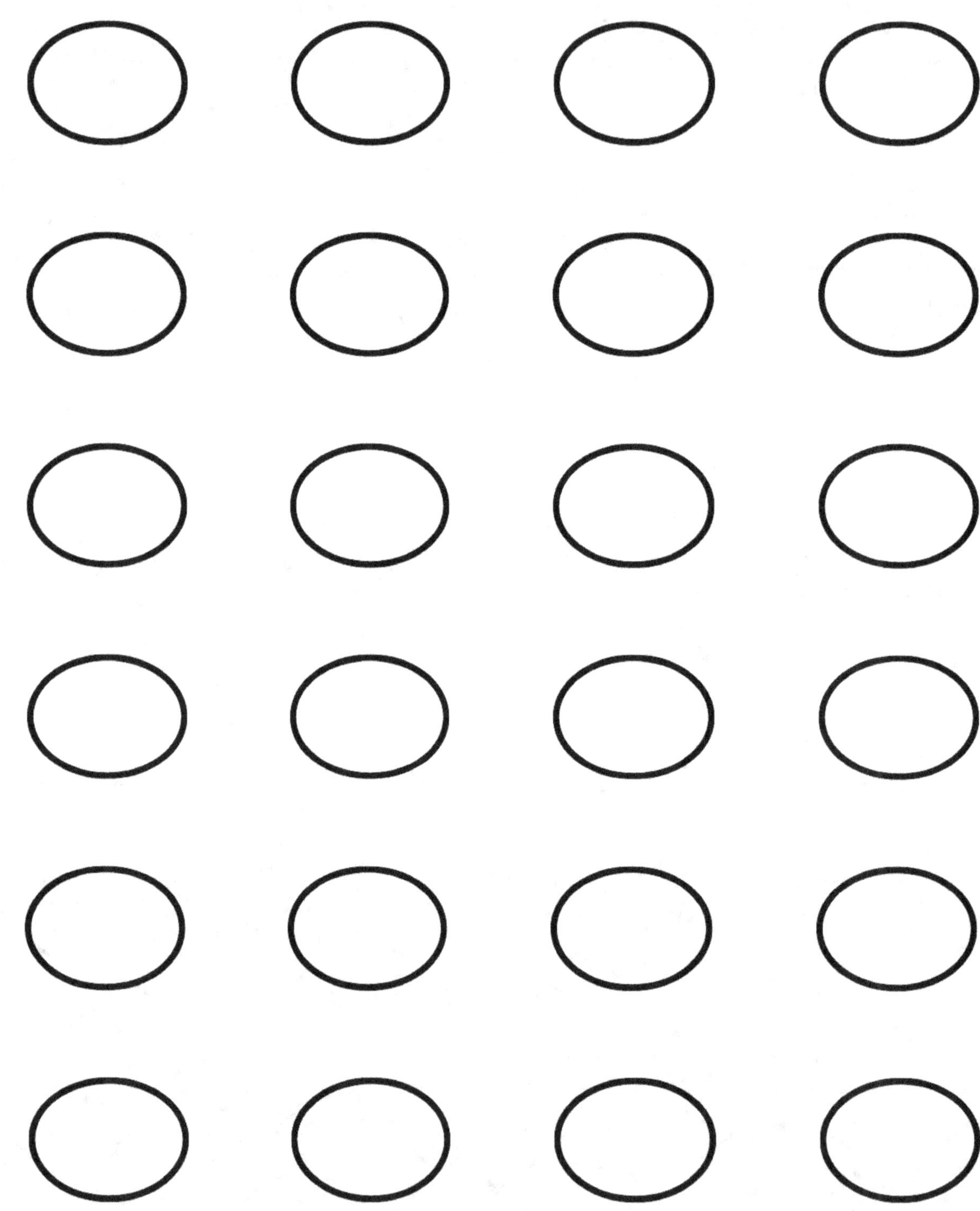

Test Color

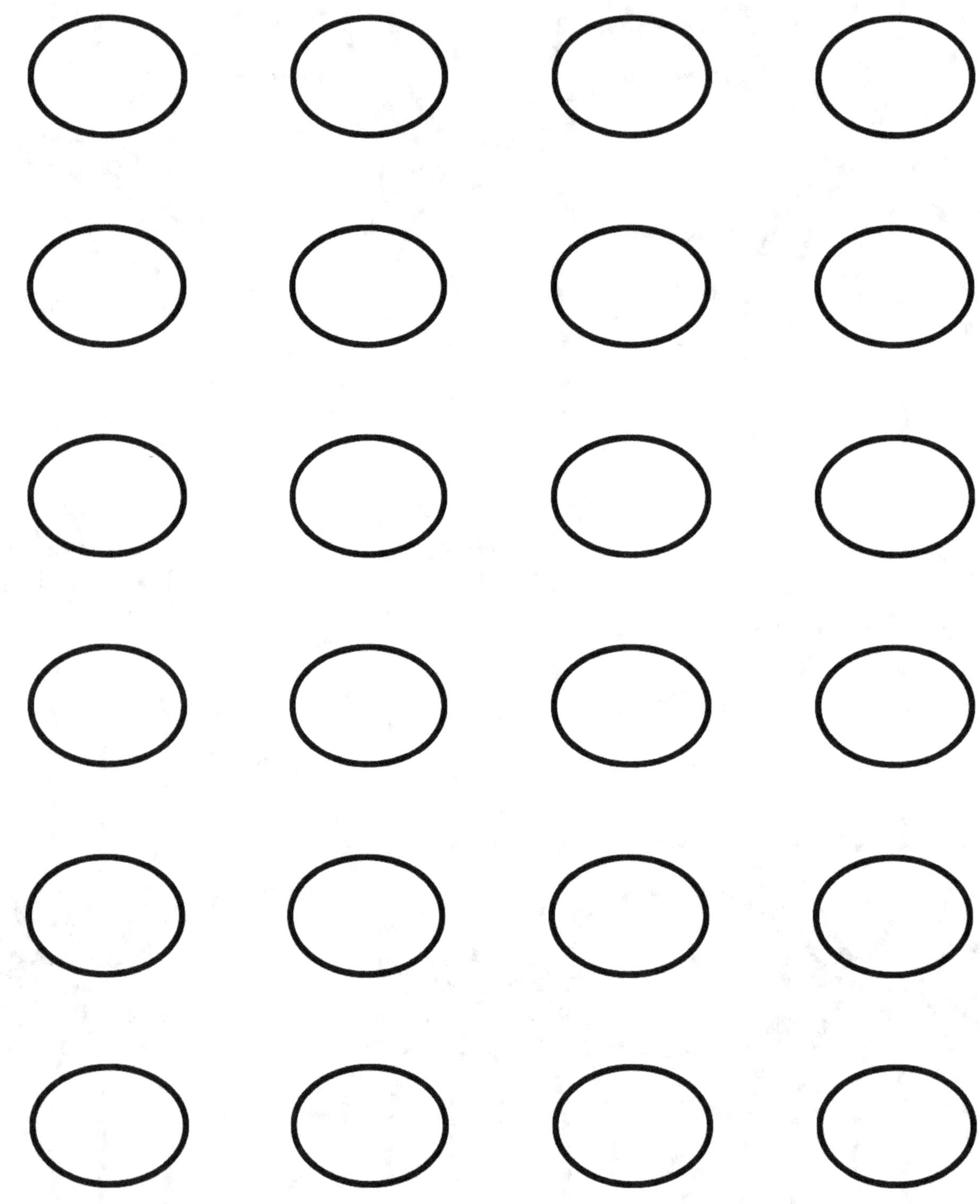

Test Color

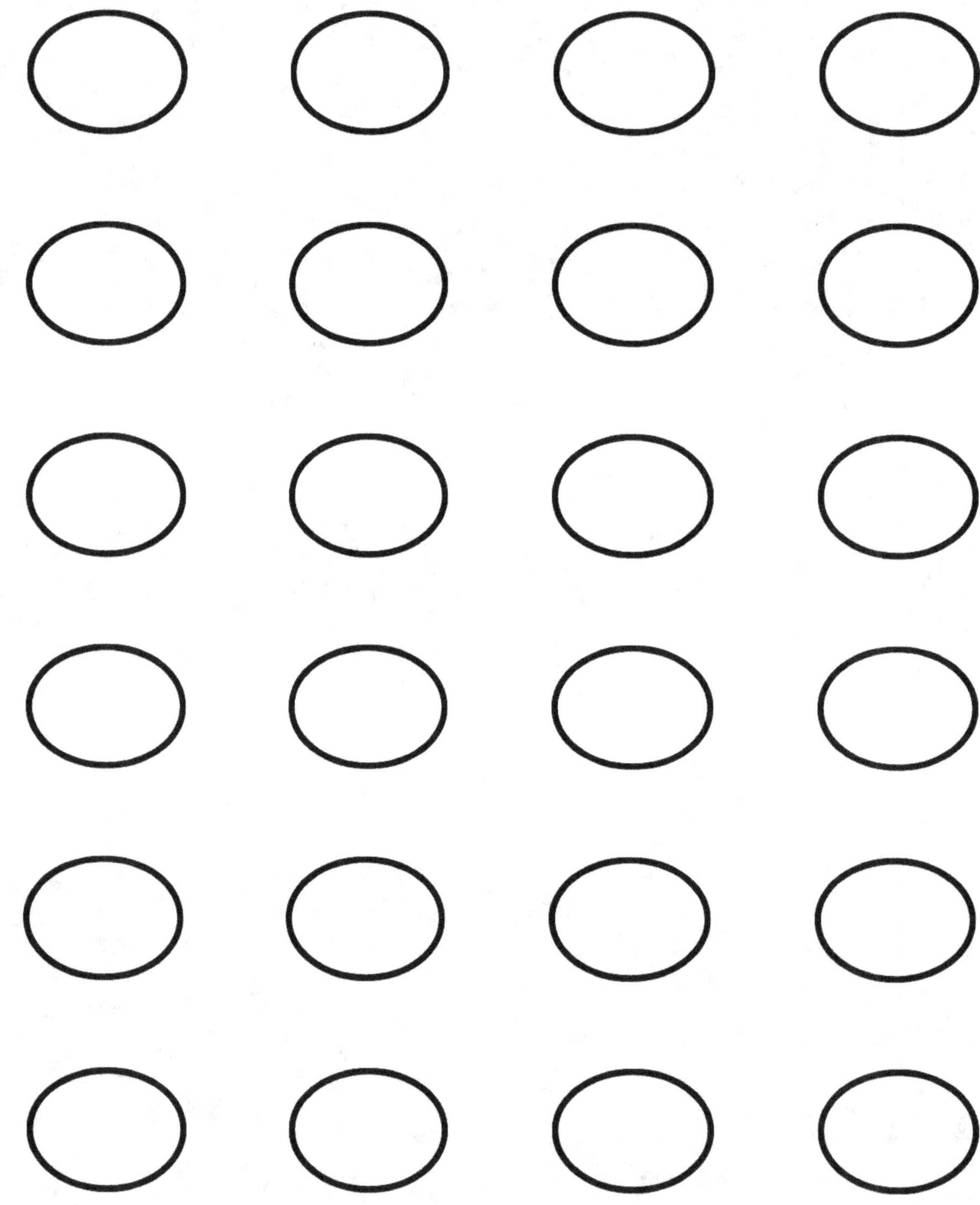

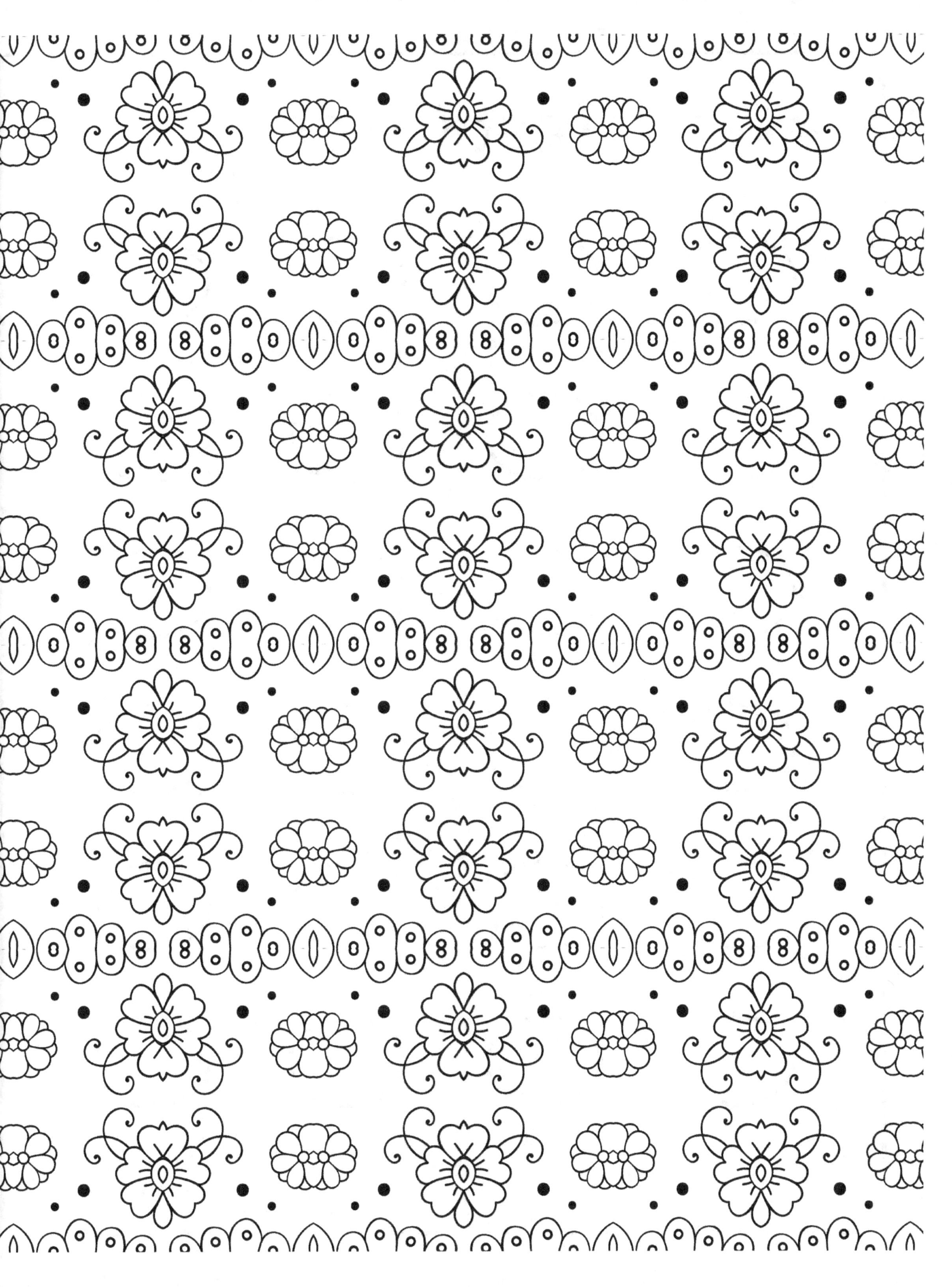

Test Color

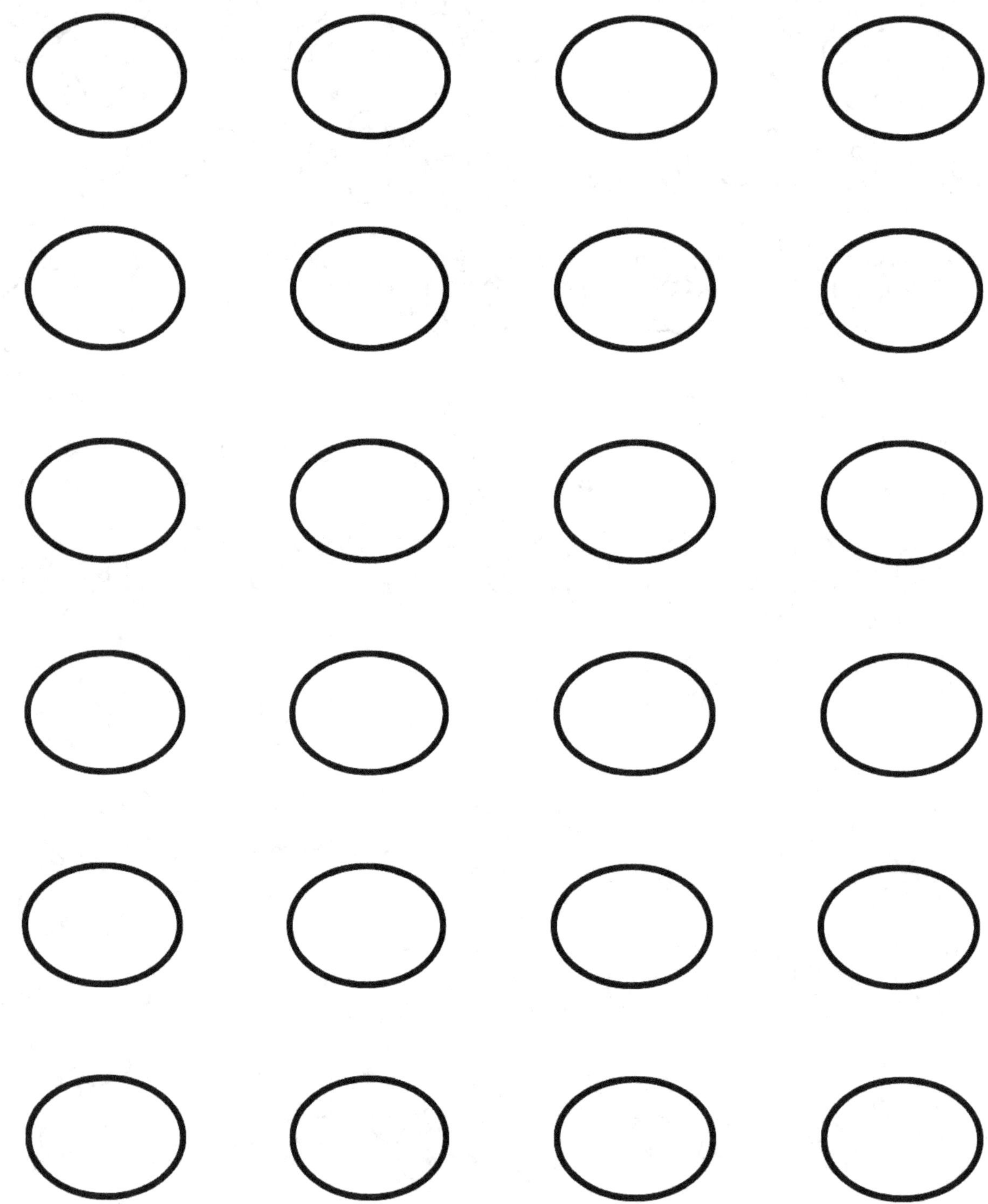

Test Color

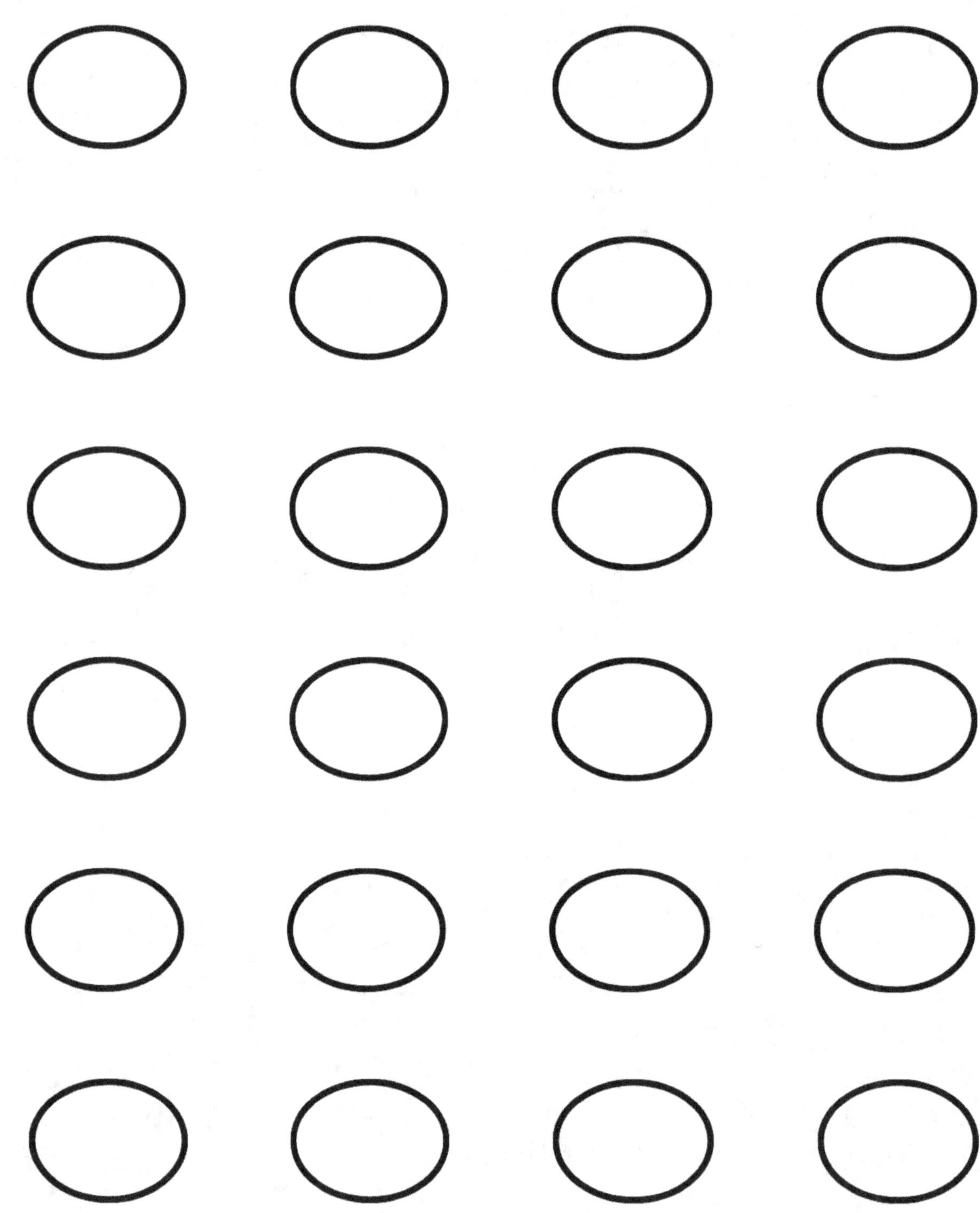

Test Color

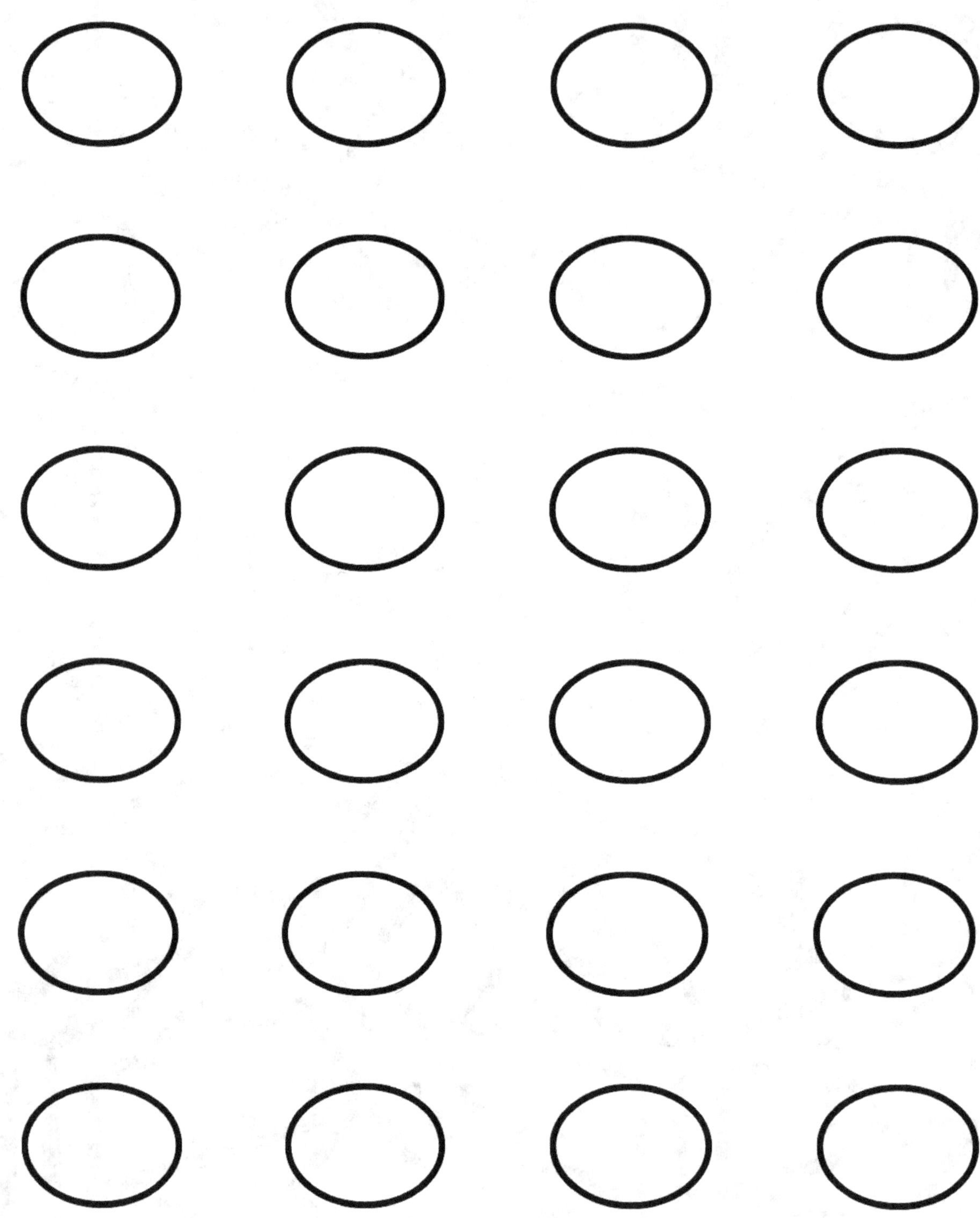

Test Color

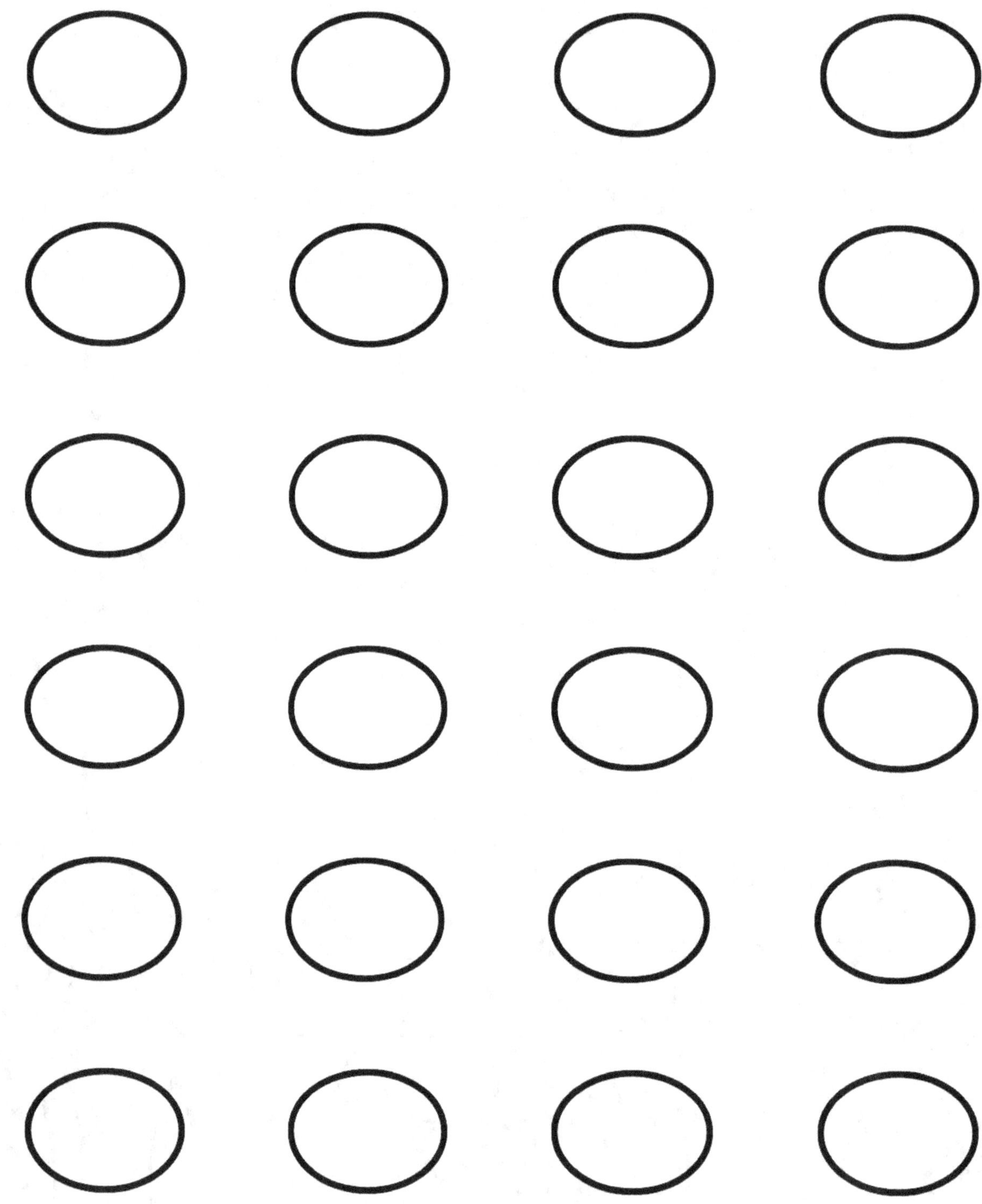

Test Color

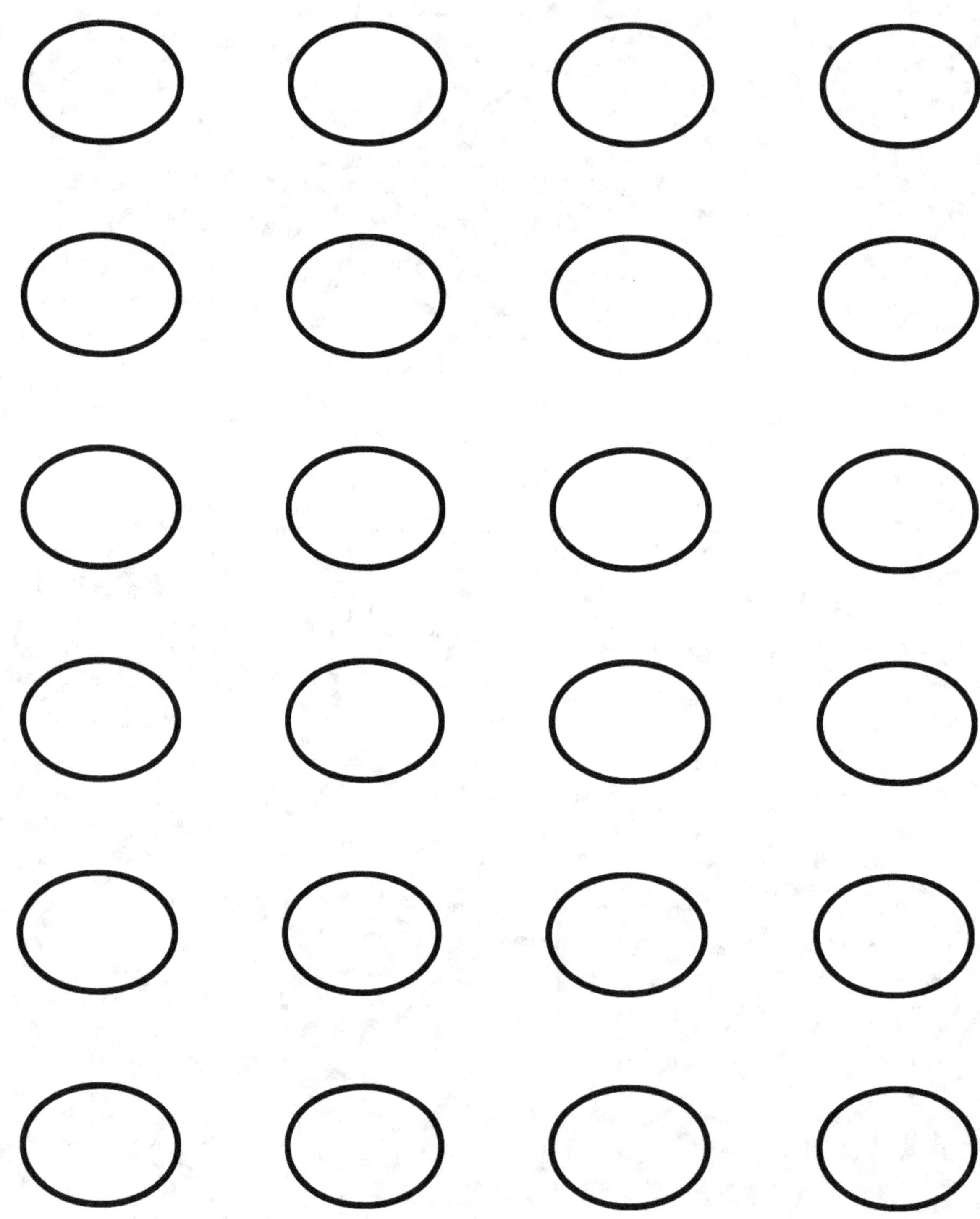

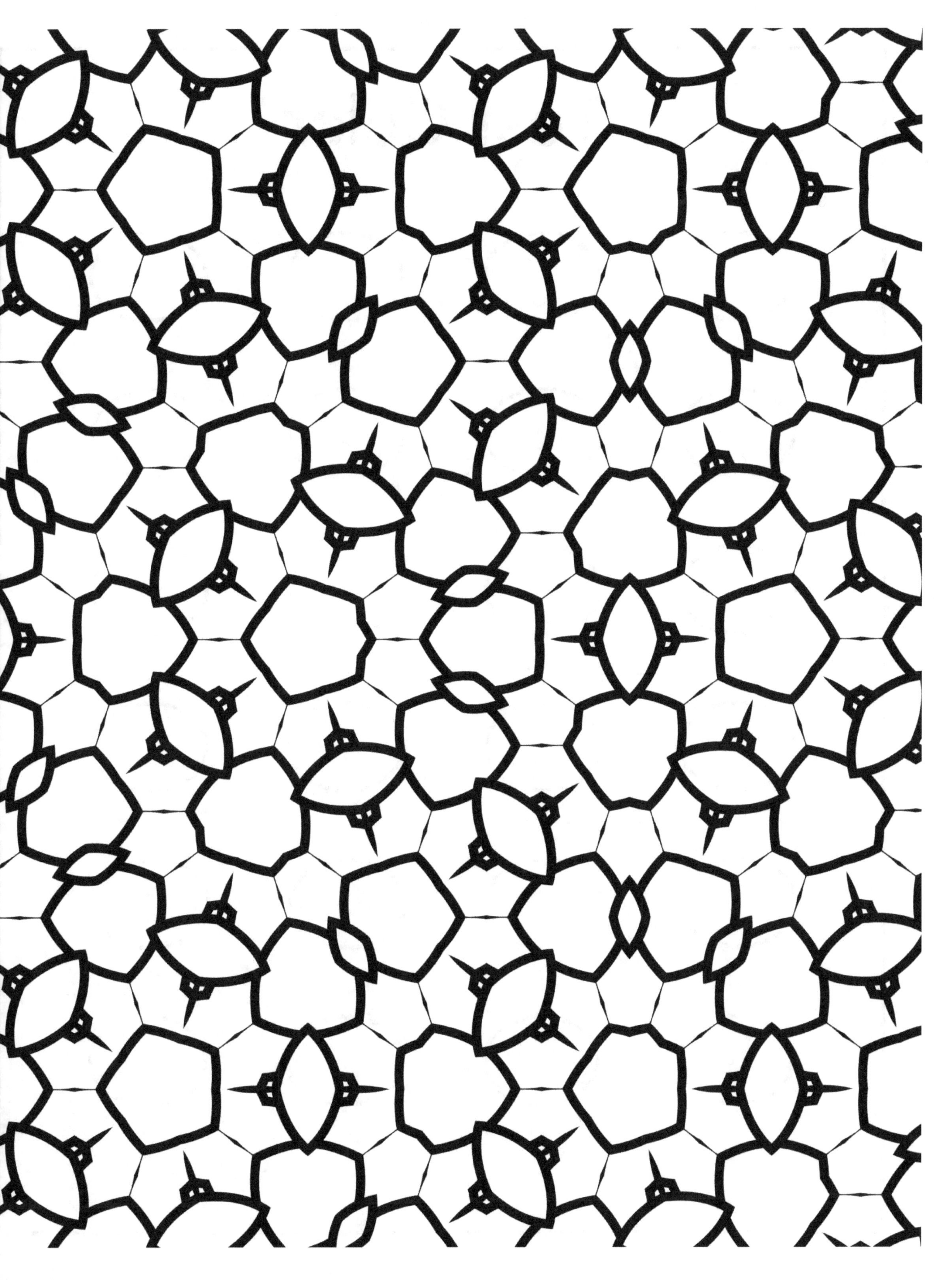

Test Color

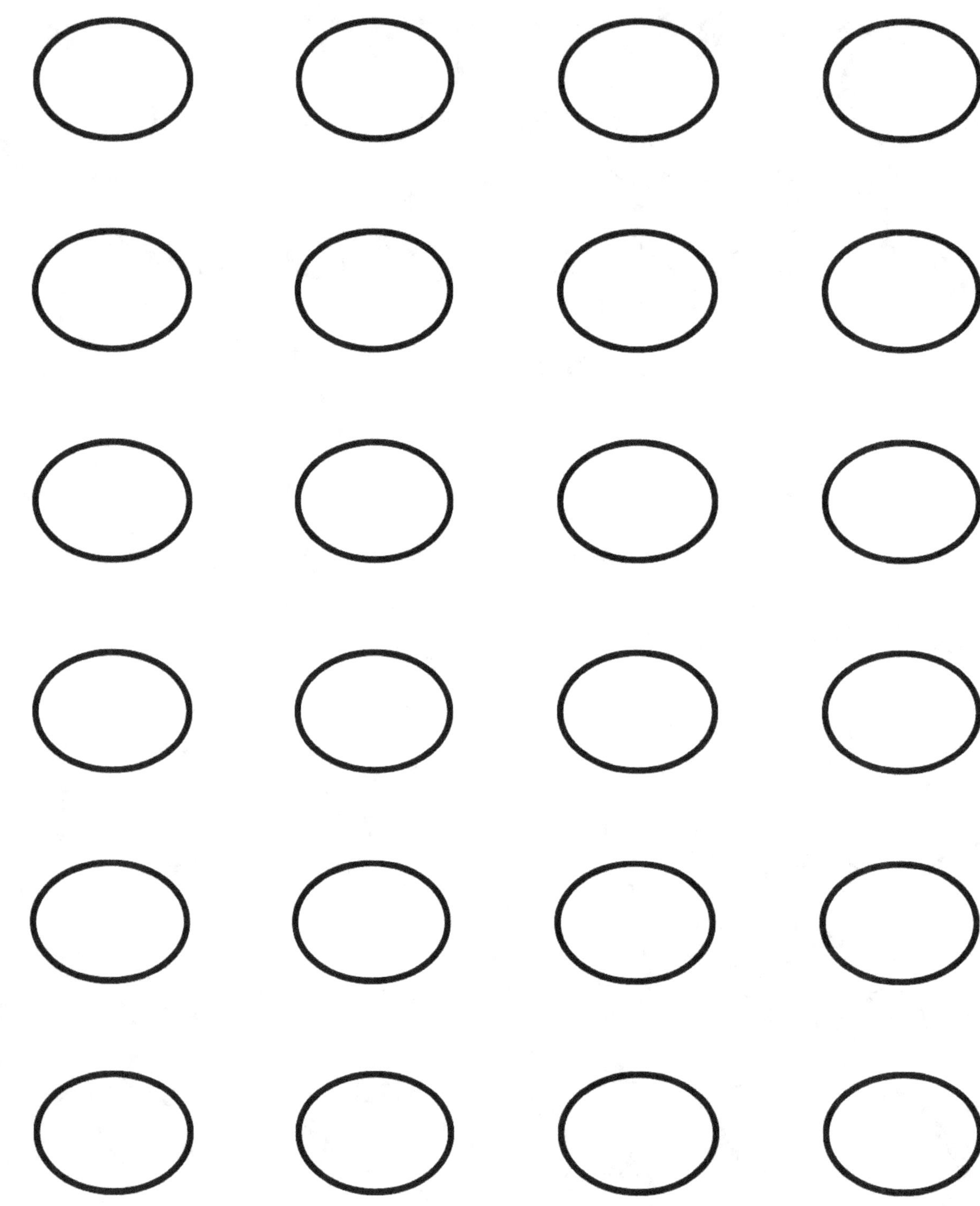

Test Color

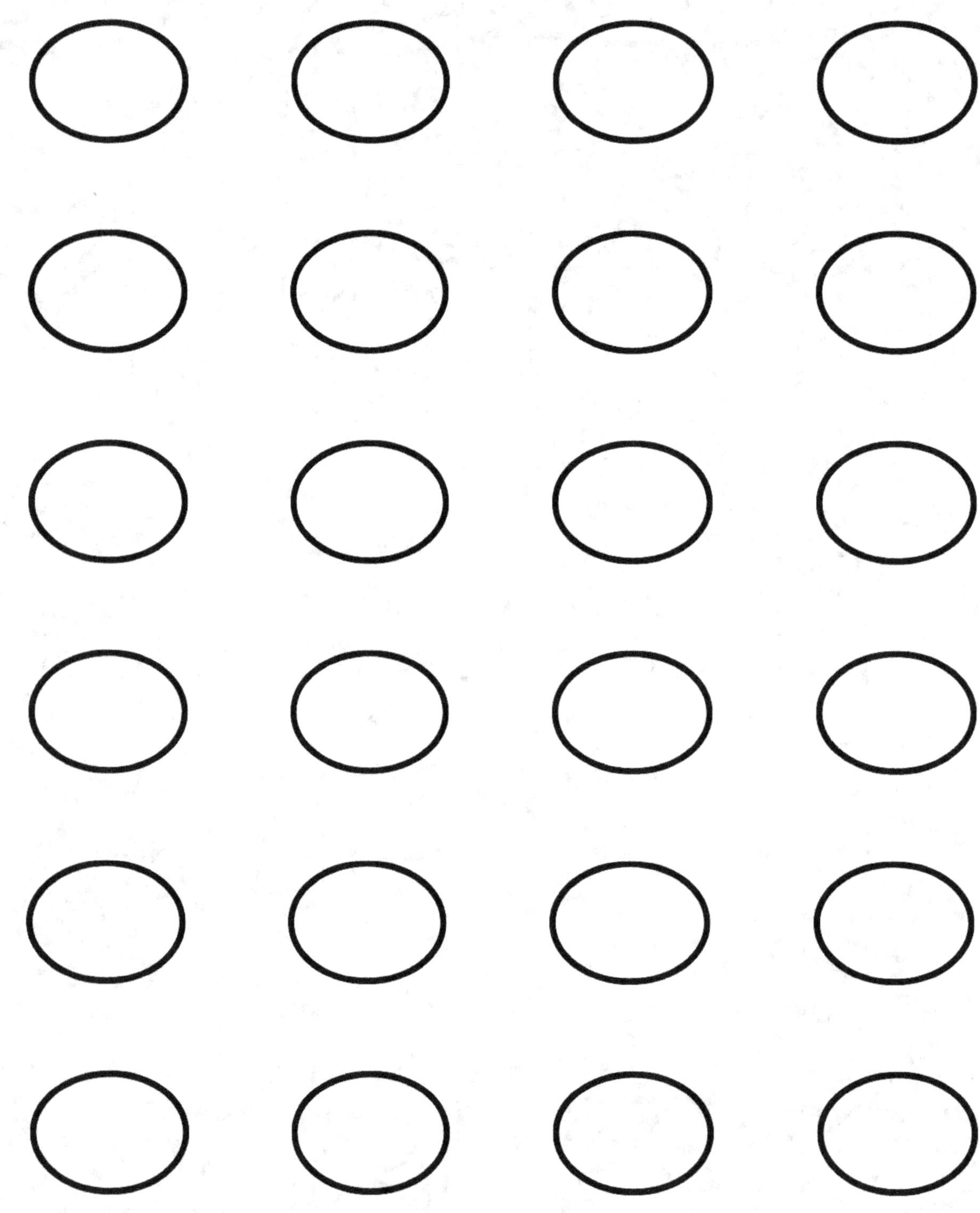

Test Color

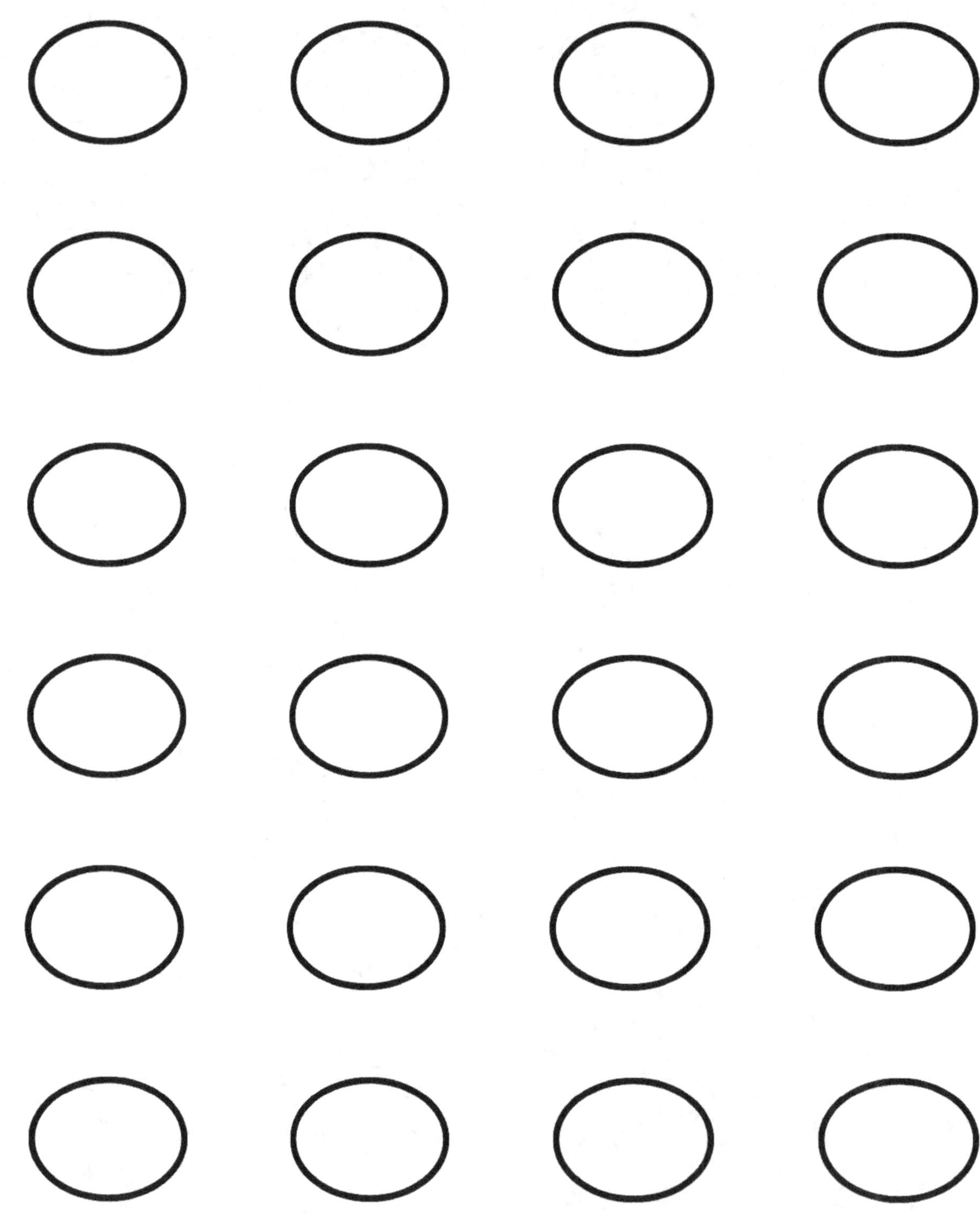

Test Color

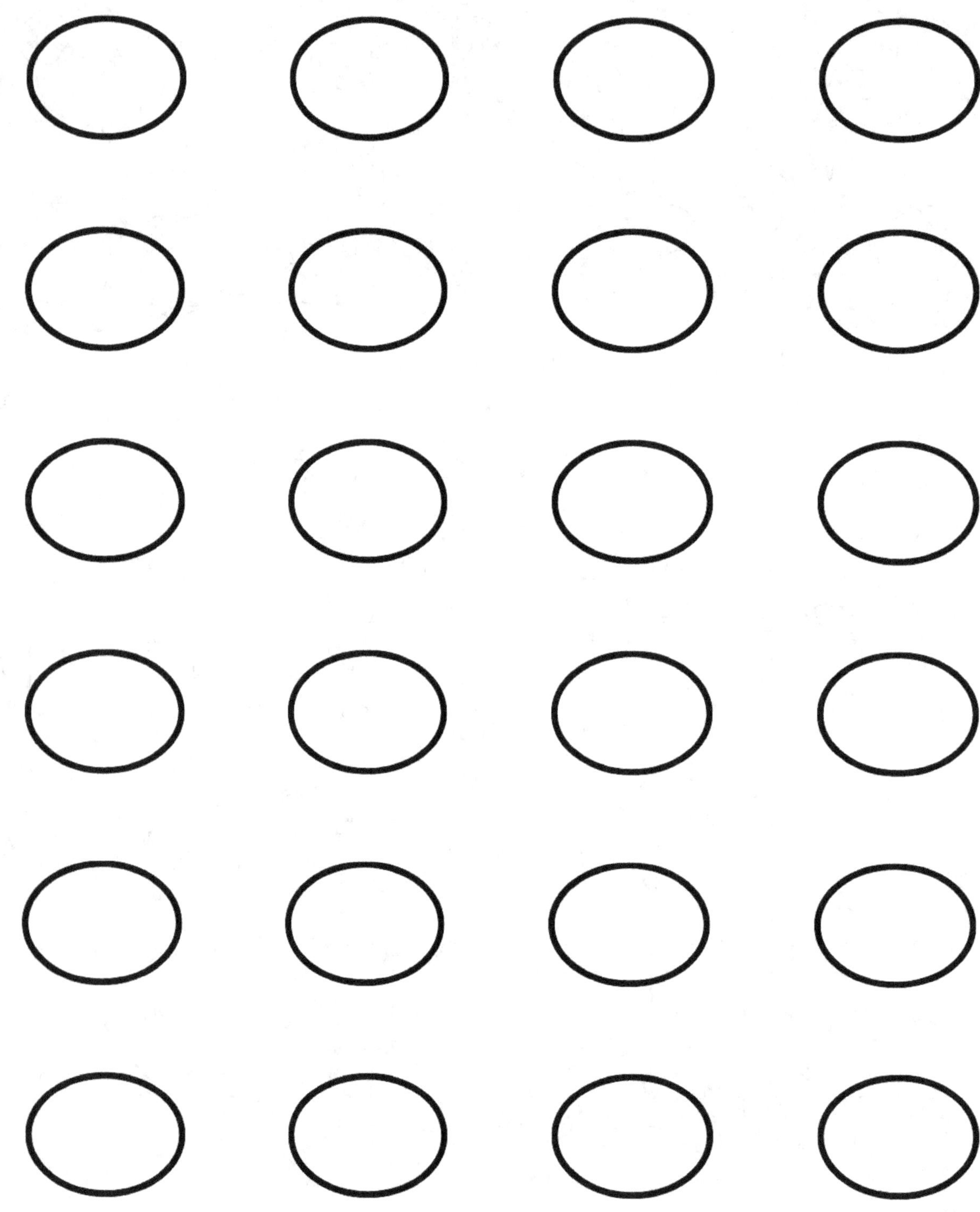

Test Color

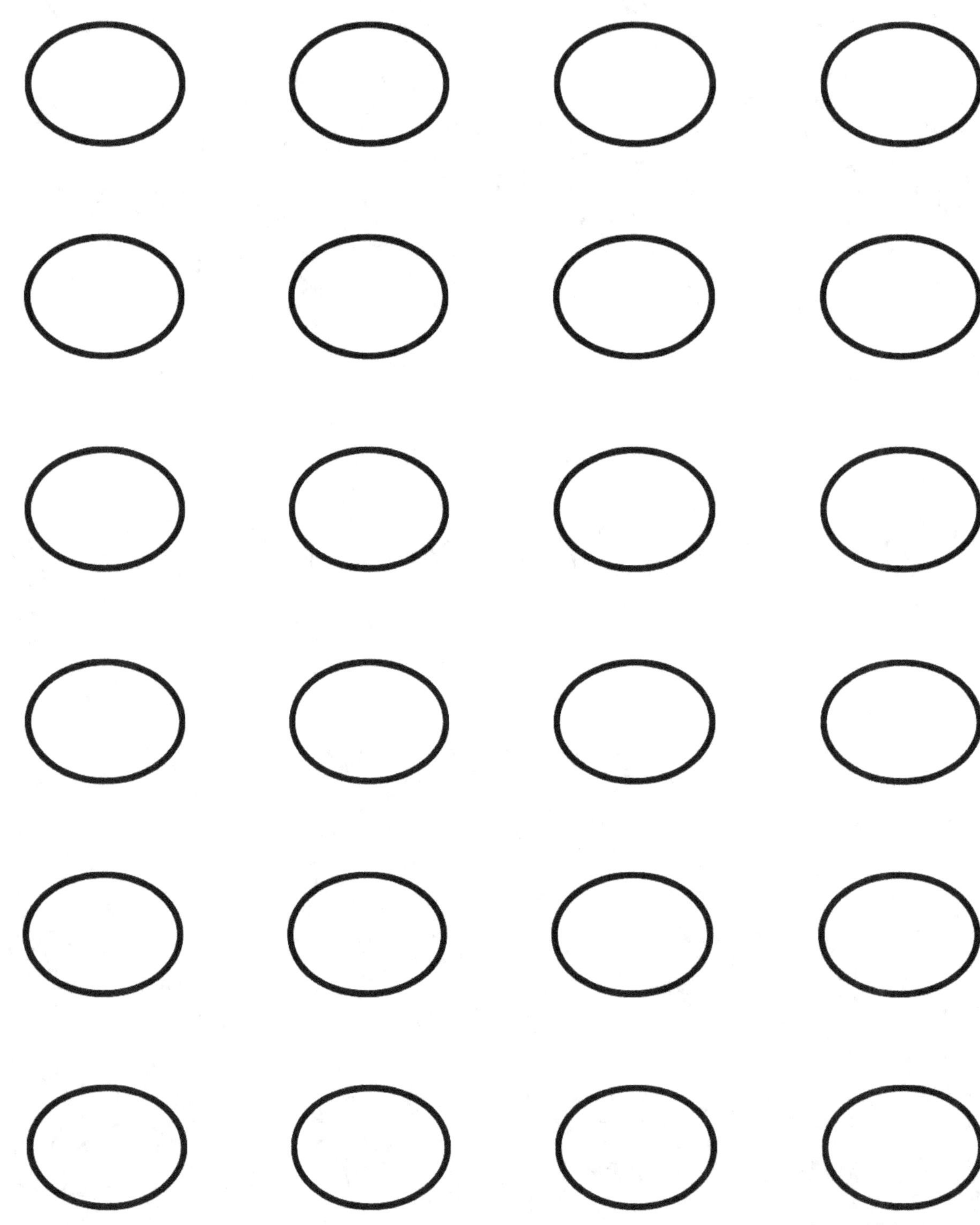

Test Color

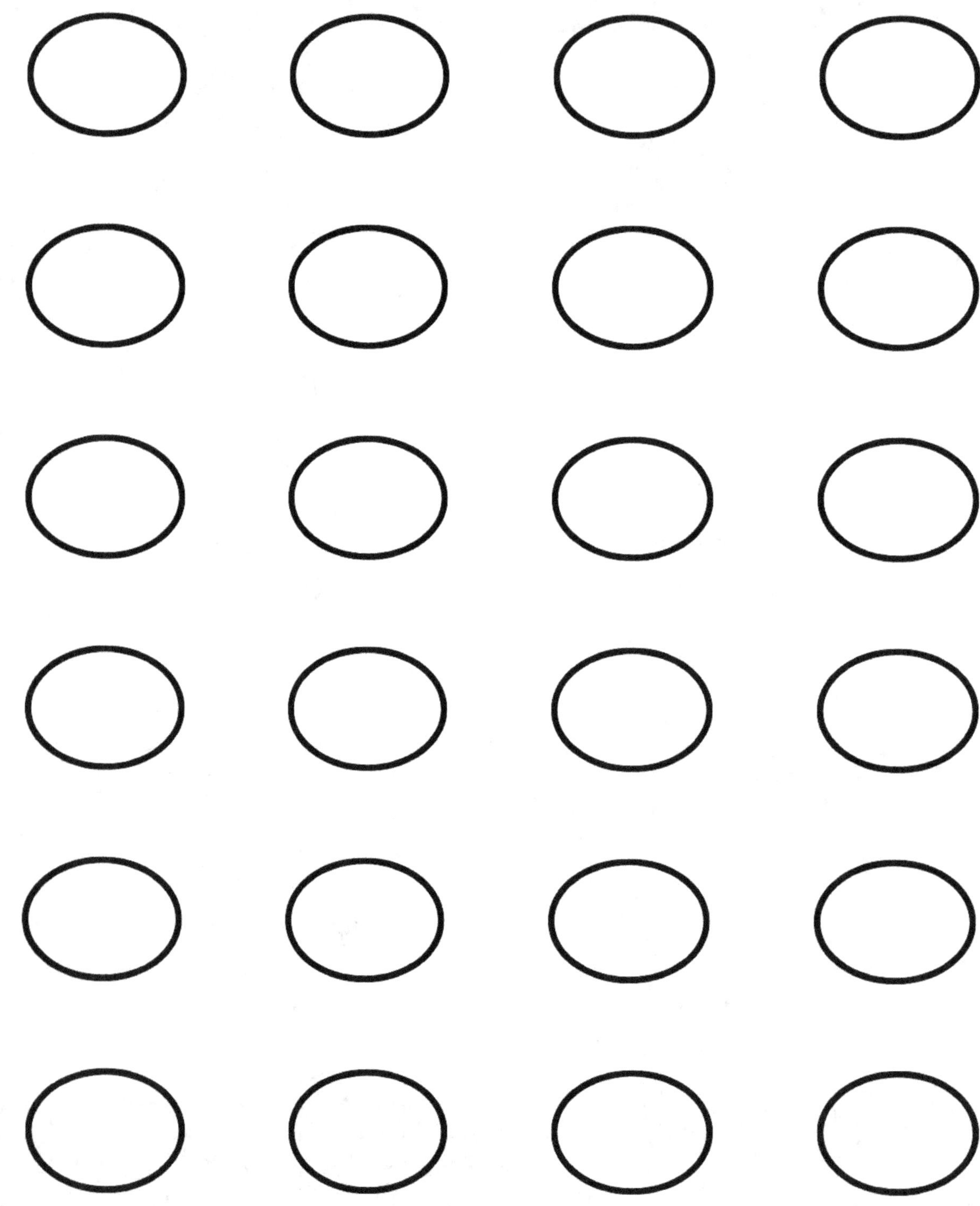

Test Color

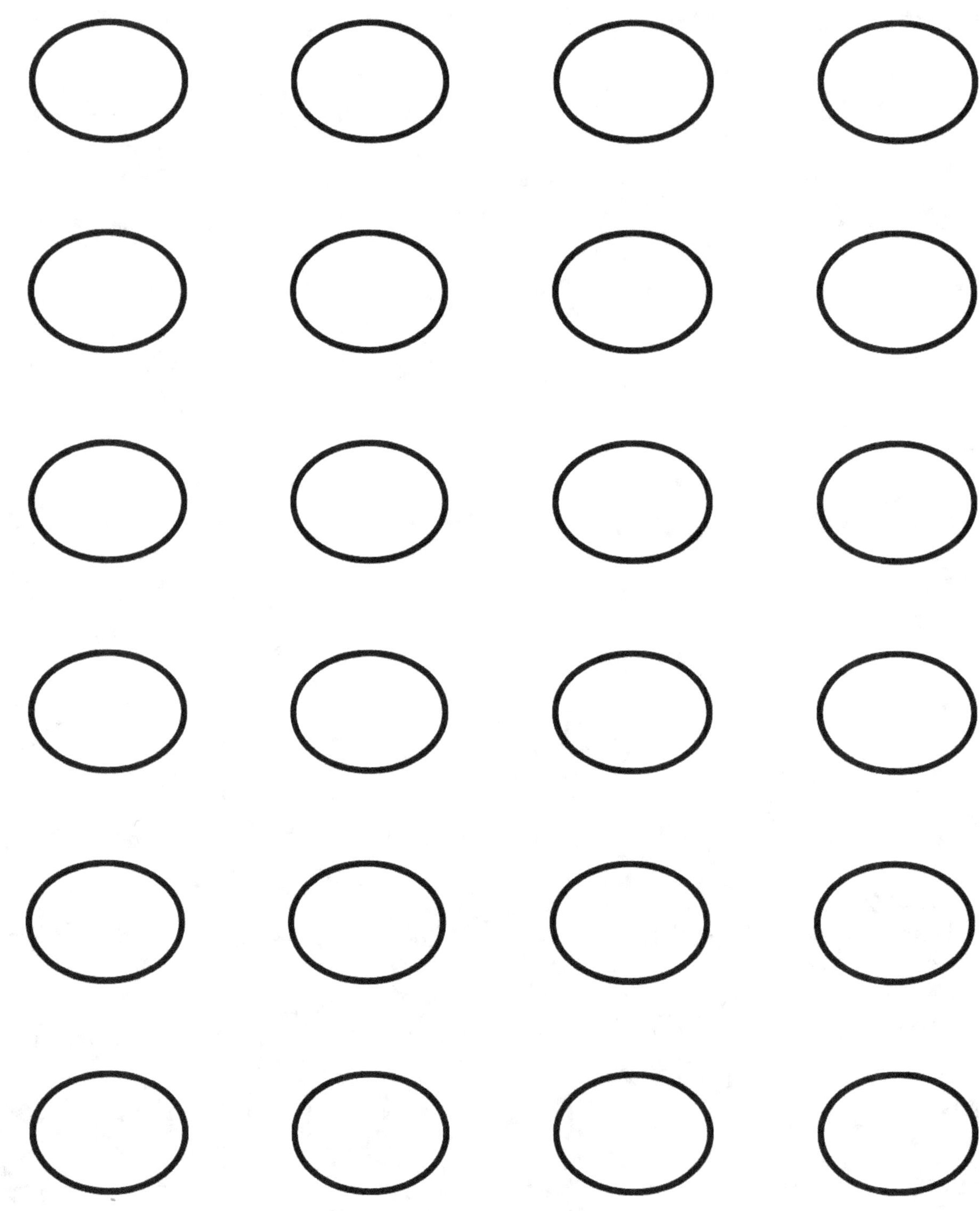

Test Color

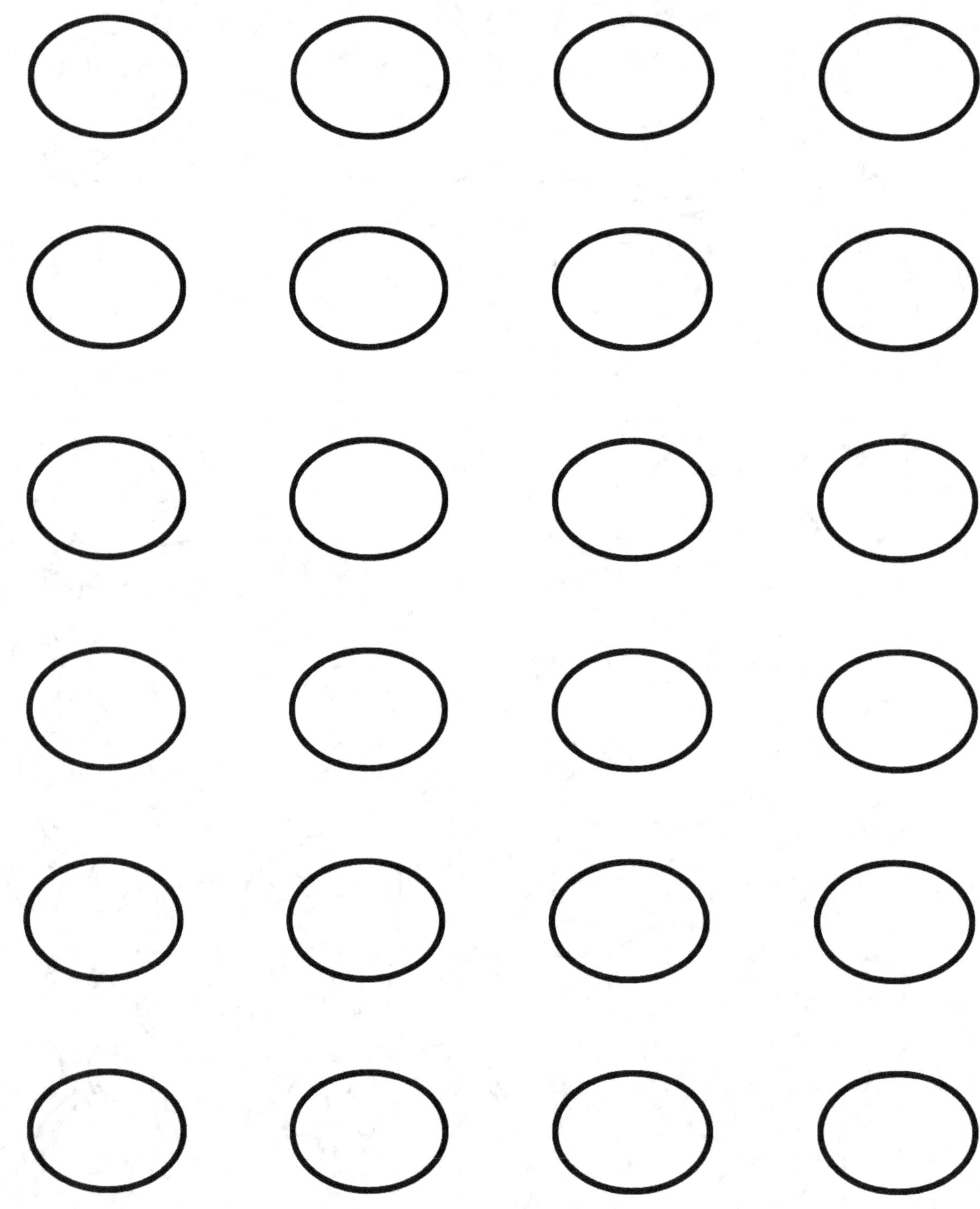